# THE CASE AGAINST WAL-MART

## Al Norman

I pledge my income
to The Store
of the United States of Wal-Mart,
and to the stockholders
for whom it expands.
One workforce,
under-paid,
with Barbie Dolls
and cheap underwear
for all.

**Raphel Marketing**

118 South Newton Place   Atlantic City, NJ  08401

*"Behind every great fortune there is a crime."*
— Honore de Balzac

# Table of Contents

Pre -Trial Arguments:  A Chain of Exploitation     v

Count 1:    Abuse of Power     1

Count 2:    Destroying the Value of Labor     5

Count 3:    Exploiting Your Suppliers     27

Count 4:    Degrading the Environment     37

Count 5:    Unfair Competition     43

Count 6:    Questionable Banking Practices     69

Count 7:    Exploiting  Global Trade     73

Count 8:    Corporate Welfare Abuse     87

Count 9:    Charity: False Advertising     101

Count 10:    Danger to Public Safety     111

Count 11:    Abandonment of Premises     115

Count 12:    Crime: Reckless Endangerment     123

Count 13:    Injurious To Private Property     135

Instructions to the Jury:  A Shopper's Boycott     145

# Acknowledgments

The author would like to thank Josie Norman, Kate Norman and Omar Frometa for their support and encouragement during my prolonged absence from their lives while distracted by this book. Thanks to Winter Miller for her copy editing, and for her audacious offer to clean up my office.

Thanks to Janis Raye for her assistance with editing, and to Neil Raphel — not only for his final editing of this work — but for his commitment to taking on a powerful corporation that other publishers would never confront, or turn away for lack of profit.

Thanks to my wife Anna Morrison for being far too forgiving of my obsession with getting out this story of corporate America.

Finally, let me thank all the "accidental activists" across the country who inspired this fight, and who town-by-town have proven that the First Amendment is a force capable of tripping giants.

**To Anna Morrison**

# Pre-Trial Arguments:
# A Chain of Exploitation

*"I will openly say I don't like Wal-Mart. I have a personal philosophy that
they have done more damage to small-town America than any other large entity."*
— City Councilman Tim Owens, Overland Park, Kansas, February 2001

In 1993, when I was first asked to fight Wal-Mart in my hometown
of Greenfield, Massachusetts, my blunt reaction was, "Why? Who cares?
It's just a place to get cheap underwear."

We had one Wal-Mart about twenty miles away in New Hampshire,
but I had never set foot in the store. Frankly, I saw no compelling reason
to get involved. I had been asked to run a voter's campaign to challenge a
rezoning that would pave the way for Wal-Mart. If the voters were with us,
Wal-Mart would lose. We had to reverse a vote of our Town Council to turn
industrial land on the edge of town into commercial land for Wal-Mart.

"How long is this campaign going to last?" I asked.

"Thirteen weeks," I was told.

"Fine," I said. "For thirteen weeks, it's fine."

But more than a decade later, I am more embroiled in the Wal-Mart
issue than I ever imagined.

Simply put, the more I learned about Wal-Mart, the less I liked.

What I discovered was that this chain store from Arkansas was
really a chain of exploitation that stretched from the sweatshops in China
to the sales floors in California. All along the chain, each link represented
the pain and suffering of thousands of people — some workers, some
consumers, some suppliers. Each link in the retailing process was forged
in the heat of unfair advantage, abuse, and deception.

This book details "The Case Against Wal-Mart."

This is a company that owns no means of production. It claims
plausible deniability for all the wrongs committed in its name. Wal-Mart's

CEO can watch videos of children in hellish sweatshops making their corporate brand, and still say, "I am comfortable with what we have done."

This is a company that makes money on life insurance when its employees die.

This is a company where more than half of its workers leave every year.

This is a company that calls "full-time" 28 hours a week.

This is a company that was sued by its own workers for forcing them to labor "off the clock" without pay.

This is a company whose goal is to make its competitors "eat dust," leaving the local economy in shambles.

This is a company whose founder wrote a book called *Made in America*, yet became the largest importer of Chinese goods in the world.

This is a company that would conceal crime at its stores, and fight the victims of such crime in court.

This is a company that sells knock-off goods and counterfeit merchandise that confuse and mislead the consumer.

This is a company that is sued more often than any other private company in the country.

This is a company that pollutes rivers, and leaves hundreds of empty stores across the country like cast-off children.

This is a company that says it promotes competition yet refuses to lease its empty stores to discounters, warehouse clubs or pharmacies.

This is a company that boasts of its charitable giving to drive sales higher.

This is a company that frequently seeks corporate welfare from taxpayers, while making billions in profits.

This is a company that says it will not go where it is not wanted, then locates its stores in the middle of quiet neighborhoods, ruining the daily life of thousands of homeowners around the country.

This is a company that injures thousands of shoppers every year from falling merchandise — and then fights them in court.

All of these charges form the case against Wal-Mart.

To many Americans, the jury is still out on Wal-Mart.

You can sift through the evidence provided in this book, and weigh the guilt or innocence of this company.

The verdict is in your hands.

# Count 1:
# Abuse of Power

*"Becoming the world's largest retailer was never considered.
And being big has never been the goal."*
— Wal-Mart's 1996 Annual Report

## The Wal-Martian Invasion

America has been invaded by Wal-Martians. They have successfully colonized the United States, and planted their flag in nine other nations.

It did not happen overnight, and it was not the lead story on the 6 o'clock news. It happened incrementally, over the past four decades. The founder of this corporate-nation, Sam Walton, was 44 years old before he opened his first Wal-Mart. His wife, Helen, had told him, "I'll go with you any place you want so long as you don't ask me to live in a big city. Ten thousand people is enough for me." The Waltons began opening stores in small southern towns, and forty-two years later, the founder has passed on, his wife is one of the richest women in the world, and their company has a workforce nearly three times larger than the U.S. Army. "Will we all work for Wal-Mart?" asks Geoffrey Colvin in a November 2003 issue of *Fortune* magazine.

Wal-Mart's growth has been amazing. It is hard to really comprehend how big Wal-Mart is today and how fast the company is still growing. In 1986, the company had net sales of $8.45 billion. Four years later, in 1990, Wal-Mart's net sales had tripled to $25.8 billion. By 1995, sales had more than tripled again to $82.49 billion, and by the year 2000, sales had doubled to $165 billion.

In 2003, Wal-Mart reached $244.5 billion in sales. Between 1986 and 1996, Wal-Mart's net sales increases averaged 27.6% a year. By 2003, Wal-Mart sales were 28 times larger than in 1986. In 1986, the company

1

had 882 discount stores and Sam's Clubs in the U.S. The company had not yet entered into its supercenter phase, nor had any international stores. By 2003, its U.S. store count was 3,400 stores, plus 1,288 international stores. The company had five times as many stores as it had 17 years earlier.

In this same time span, the headcount of Wal-Mart employees grew from 104,000 to 1,400,000. The number of stockholders increased fifteen-fold, from 21,828 to 330,000. By far, much of the company's stratospheric growth took place after founder Sam Walton died in 1992. The company today is more than five times larger than it was at Walton's death, and employs four times as many people.

Much of this "growth" actually has been just a shift in market share — money "captured" from other merchants. Economists call this "transferred sales." The "lesser chains" that Wal-Mart replaced were less efficient, less focused than Wal-Mart. Their significance may lie not in their mediocrity or shortcomings, but in the hole they left, rather than the hole they filled while still open. As merchants closed up shop, they took with them the kind of diverse local players needed for competition to thrive.

Take the grocery industry, for example. Wal-Mart had a very small share of a very diversified grocery market ten years ago. Today, Wal-Mart and Sam's Club control 19% of grocery sales. In addition to its dominant position in the domestic grocery industry, Wal-Mart also now controls a staggering 50% of all grocery sales in Mexico. When Wal-Mart Mexico's three largest grocery competitors in Mexico announced in July of 2003 that they were going to combine forces to compete with the gringo giant, their total sales combined were still less than Wal-Mart's.

The "one nation, one store" concept is rapidly metastasizing into a "one world, one store" reality. Wal-Mart's modus operandi for going global has been to buy up shares of indigenous companies in other countries. Wal-Mart bought up existing merchants in Mexico, England, Germany and Japan. In England, Wal-Mart purchased the ASDA chain, and by August 2003, had become the second largest grocer in the United Kingdom. In March 2002, Wal-Mart announced it had purchased a "strategic stake" in the Seiyu Ltd. company, an $8 billion Japanese retail chain. Foreign sales from countries like England, Germany and China make an increasingly important mix of sales for Wal-Mart. The cover of the company's 2000 Annual Report featured employees holding up flags from Germany and Mexico with the slogan: "Banner Year for International

Expansion." By February 2003, international sales accounted for 17% of Wal-Mart's total sales, or more than $40 billion in sales. Globalization has been a double win for Wal-Mart: they import more cheap goods into the U.S., and they open international markets for those goods.

More than eight years ago, Wal-Mart's sales surpassed the Gross Domestic Product of Israel, Greece, Ireland and Egypt. A Price Waterhouse report noted that by the year 2005, just 10 companies, including Wal-Mart, will control 50% of food store sales. The United Food and Commercial Workers went further. At their 2003 annual convention in San Francisco, union leaders warned that Wal-Mart planned to add 800,000 new workers over the next five years, and that Wal-Mart would control 50% of the retail food market in the United States by 2008.

This suggests that Wal-Mart represents not the beginning of competition — but the end of competition in America. According to an International Council of Shopping Centers report in 1998:

> Numerous store types that are key elements in U.S. shopping centers are dominated by a small group of retailers in each category that register a third or more of their respective category's total U.S. sales…as fewer firms exercise increasing sales dominance within their respective store types…the pricing power that will accrue to the largest retailers will likely make it difficult for large numbers of new, small operators to take root and thrive.

The symptoms of retail saturation are everywhere. As of 1999, America had:

- More than 4,000 abandoned shopping malls in America.
- More shopping centers than high schools.
- 20 square feet of retail space for every man, woman and child in America, an increase from 14.7 square feet per person in 1986. By contrast, Britain had only 2 square feet of retail space per person.

Even the people who produce all this sprawl admit that we have more retail stores than our disposable income can absorb. Tom Seay, Wal-Mart's former Vice President for Real Estate in a 1996 court deposition admitted, "We have more shopping center space in the U.S.

than is needed. We're in an over-built situation."

When Wal-Mart says "one stop shopping," we should read that statement very literally. At the end of Wal-Mart TV commercials, the company ran the words: "Next stop home." In 1994, a retail analyst at the consulting firm Management Horizons made this tongue-in-cheek prediction about Wal-Mart:

> If Wal-Mart grows in the next eight years as it has in the previous eight, it will control 100% of general merchandise sales in the United States; if it grows in the next 16 years as it has in the previous 16 years, it will control all of the non-auto retailing volume in the United States; if the same growth pattern for the next 24 years is like the previous 24 years, Wal-Mart will control all of the country's Gross Domestic Product.

The size and clout of Wal-Mart has become a direct threat to the free marketplace, where competitive price depends on a diverse number of relatively equal players. As the weaker players die off, including some very large regional and national chain stores, competition in the market is weakened, and the consumer suffers.

Welcome to the United States of Wal-Mart. One nation. One store. For all.

# Count 2:
# Destroying the Value of Labor

*"Seniority and doing a good job mean nothing here. The Wal-Mart Open Door policy means that if you open your mouth, you'll be out the door."*
- Dale Stiles, Wal-Mart employee, *Arkansas Times,* September 1992

## Sub-count A:  Dead-End Jobs

In every Wal-Mart employee's handbook, workers are told that "one of the main foundations of our people philosophy is that our people make the difference. This belief carries over to everything we do." The company says its employees are all on a first name basis. "This helps promote the warm, friendly atmosphere our customers and associates have come to expect."

It must give Wal-Mart a warm, friendly feeling to know that in 2003 it made roughly $5,742 in net profit from each of its "associates."

In the summer of 2003, Wal-Mart began running TV spots that highlighted Wal-Mart workers. The focus of the ads was that Wal-Mart was a great place to work. "They give you opportunity to advance," one worker says, urging her daughter to give Wal-Mart a try. In another ad, a Wal-Mart district manager with two children says, "It's not easy to have a career and a family, but my job makes it a lot easier to do both."

According to *The New York Times*, the ads were produced by a Texas advertising company "to reverse criticism [that] many people view Wal-Mart as a place of dead-end jobs." The newspaper said the giant retailer had become "increasingly concerned about its public image." With good reason. A Bloomberg News report in November 1999 said that Wal-Mart conducted a study of its own workforce and found that almost 50% of those who quit Wal-Mart leave within the first three months on the job.

Wal-Mart denied that its TV spots had anything to do with lawsuits brought against the behemoth by its own workers, but noted that the company had engaged in a two-year process of "reputation research," that included focus groups and telephone interviews. The study found that Wal-Mart workers did not give the company good marks for pay or benefit levels.

"This is a good place to work," Coleman Peterson told *Business Week* recently. Peterson is Wal-Mart's executive vice president for personnel. He boasted that Wal-Mart's turnover rate had improved from 70% in 1999 to 45% in 2003. Even at that lower rate 630,000 people in America wearing Wal-Mart vests will quit their jobs this year. If Wal-Mart is such a "good place to work," why are an average of 52,500 employees per month leaving their jobs? Wal-Mart is not only the nation's largest private employer; it also holds the record for most employee turnover.

For years, organized labor has criticized the "everyday low wage" mentality at Wal-Mart, and an increasingly sharp-edged struggle has been waged between the unions on one side, and Wal-Mart on the other.

In San Leandro, California, Wal-Mart distributed a list of FAQ's (frequently asked questions) about the company's policies:

> Q: We have heard that Wal-Mart is anti-union. Is this true?
> A: No. Wal-Mart stores are non-union, not anti-union. Wal-Mart is pro-associate and is considered one of the top 100 companies to work for in America . . . The company also offers a work environment that encourages the freedom to communicate openly and share ideas. Wal-Mart Associates like what the company has to offer and have chosen not to unionize.

Wal-Mart was so fearful of union contact with their "associates" that the company went to great lengths to keep the two groups separated. Just before Christmas of 1999, Wal-Mart managers across the nation gave groups like the Salvation Army and the Girl Scouts a sudden "heave ho-ho-ho" right out of their store, because the world's largest retailer uncovered an insidious plot on the part of American organized workers to infiltrate the ranks of Wal-Mart workers.

It's not that Wal-Mart didn't like the Girl Scouts, or the local Police and Fire Departments — but the company said it just could not allow such groups to solicit for funds inside the store any more, because the UFCW (United Food and Commercial Workers) wanted to be inside the store too. Wal-Mart claimed to have obtained an "internal memo" from the UFCW in which the union instructed its members to document with photos and sample handouts the fact that Wal-Mart regularly allowed many organizations to "solicit inside and in front of its stores," but barred the union from doing so. According to the "internal memo," the UFCW planned to use such evidence to ask the courts for an injunction seeking access for all UFCW locals to the interior of Wal-Mart stores.

Wal-Mart is so terrified of union organizing, the company allegedly monitors some of its stores'phone calls and emails. Jon Lehman, a former Wal-Mart store manager, told *Bloomberg* news in February 2004 that Wal-Mart has a 60' x 60' room in Bentonville in which two dozen people with headsets conduct surveillance on calls and emails from stores, to see whether anyone is talking about union organizing. A Wal-Mart spokesperson responded by claiming that the retailer monitors calls only if stores are at risk for bomb threats. But there is no more explosive issue at Wal-Mart than the feared depth-charge of union sympathizers among its own workforce.

When meat cutters at a Texas Wal-Mart voted to unionize, the company announced several weeks later that it would no longer be cutting meat in-house, but would purchase meats already pre-cut, thus eliminating the unionized jobs from the payroll. It is a source of great pride at Wal-Mart that its workers "have chosen not to unionize."

For years, critics of the company have pointed out that Wal-Mart will talk endlessly about its "falling prices" — but never runs ads about its "everyday low wages."

A November 2000 Economic Impact Analysis paid for by Wal-Mart in the city of Bozeman, Montana examined the wage benefits at the giant retailer:

> Wal-Mart considers its specific existing wage levels at the Bozeman store to be proprietary information, and has declined to divulge that information … Furthermore, company representatives state that whenever a new store opens or an existing store expands, the company undertakes a study of area wages at competitive stores, in order to determine a wage level capable of attracting a qualified work force.

> Company representatives state that a supercenter of the

size contemplated in Bozeman typically has an annual payroll of $6,000,000 for approximately 500 employees, with a mix of 70% full-time workers and 30% part-time. Fifteen to twenty workers would be in management positions. Based on these numbers, the average annual pay per employee would be $12,000, or approximately $230 weekly.

Assuming an average of 28 hours per week (the level Wal-Mart considers minimum for full-time employment), average hourly pay for all workers would be just under $8.25. It should be noted that this is a very rough estimate, and does not differentiate between pay levels for entry-level workers and management. Unverified third-party information ... stated that experienced clerks at Wal-Mart average $7.50 per hour, in the same general range estimate.

The study compared Wal-Mart's $7.50 wage with the wages earned by United Food and Commercial Workers at unionized grocery stores in the Bozeman area, where a Category 2 Clerk with 3 years experience earned $10.54 per hour, and meat cutters earned $12 per hour.

Stan Cox, an opinion-editorial writer in Kansas, in June 2003 examined the take-home pay of a single parent with two children working full-time at a Salina, Kansas Wal-Mart, and concluded the employee "does not earn enough money to supply the family's basic needs by shopping at that same Wal-Mart." Cox estimated that a cashier at the Salina store made $6.25 an hour. After taking out the mandatory withholding from her paycheck, like Social Security and Medicare payroll taxes, this cashier, who was assumed to actually work 40 hours per week — even though 28 hours is full-time at Wal-Mart — had take-home pay of $1,016 a month. The familys monthly expenses assumed that they did all of their shopping at Wal-Mart, taking advantage of "everyday low prices." The analysis also assumed the family's expenses met an "adequate but austere" budget for a family with one parent, one pre-schooler, and one school-age child. Cox also calculated that the family had a rented, furnished apartment and a paid-up car. The U.S. Department of Agriculture "low cost food plan" was used to estimate food costs. Even gas, oil and car repairs were done at Wal-Mart prices — including a 10% employee discount. This austere budget assumed no travel outside the local area, no cable TV, no rental movies, no newspaper or magazine subscriptions—just a bare bones existence in the heartland of Kansas.

Cox concluded, "The bottom line: [a worker] would need an absolute minimum of $1,136 per month to cover housing, food, transportation, health care and miscellaneous expenses. Despite our best efforts, we exceeded our cashier's monthly income by $120." Furthermore, in calculating costs, Cox's study assumed that the family took advantage of Kansas' child-care allowance benefit, and claimed both a $4,140 earned income tax credit from the federal government and food stamps. Such workers survive only with the support of federal, and often state, taxpayers. Their subsidized employment helps to underwrite Wal-Mart's cost advantage over their so-called "competitors."

In February 2004, the Committee on Education and the Workforce of the U.S. House of Representatives released a report, "Everyday Low Wages: The Hidden Price We All Pay for Wal-Mart." Written by the Democratic staff of Congressman George Miller (D-CA), the report concludes that Wal-Mart low wages are subsidized by federal taxpayers. Because Wal-Mart does not pay its workers a living wage, U.S. taxpayers pick up the bill. A typical Wal-Mart store with 200 employees costs federal taxpayers $420,750 per year – about $2,103 per employee – in the following ways:

- $36,000 a year to pay for free and reduced lunches for Wal-Mart families
- $42,000 a year for housing assistance
- $125,000 a year for federal tax credits and deductions for low-income families
- $100,000 a year for additional child tax credits
- $108,000 a year for federal health care costs of moving into state children's health insurance programs
- $9,750 a year for the additional costs of low-income energy assistance.

The report concludes, "Wal-Mart's success has meant downward pressures on wages and benefits, rampant violations of basic worker's rights, and threats to the standard of living in communities across the country. The success of business need not come at the expense of workers and their families. Such short-sighted profit-making strategies ultimately undermine our economy."

But Wal-Mart's low wages also create a guaranteed market for its main product: cheap merchandise. At the wages Wal-Mart pays, its associates are likely to purchase their consumables at Wal-Mart, in effect recycling their salary back to the company. At 1.4 million paychecks, that's not an insubstantial amount of money returning from its own workforce.

When Wal-Mart first pitches its superstore to a community, it will talk about the "new jobs" that Wal-Mart brings. But it will not talk about the displacement of old jobs already in the community, or the cost to the community of lost manufacturing jobs. A study by the Institute for International Economics, examining U.S. manufacturing job losses from 1979 to 1999, found that one in four factory workers who lost their jobs had to accept pay cuts of 25% or more. The Brookings Institute estimates that the money these workers lost in wages when they took a lower-paying job amounted to $8 billion to $12 billion a year, according to a December 2003 article in *The New York Times*. When economists praise Wal-Mart for lowering the cost of living in America, it sounds like faint praise to the millions of factory workers whose standard of living may never recover from Wal-Mart globalization of production. Ironically, as Wal-Mart lowers the cost of a marketbasket of consumer goods, and thus the consumer price index, down with it comes the Cost of Living Adjustment that lowers the annual Social Security check for 47 million elders and disabled Americans.

Over the years, store by store, as Wal-Mart has gained an increasing market share of the discount and grocery market, a "race to the bottom" dynamic has been created, forcing down the wages and benefits of workers outside of Wal-Mart. For example, in 2002, during labor contract negotiations in Oregon, three grocery chains, Fred Meyer, Safeway and Albertsons, all cited the increasing competition for nonunion stores, such as Wal-Mart and Costco, as the impetus for concessions in health care benefits from their union employees in the United Food and Commercial Workers. According to the *Register-Guard*, a newspaper in Eugene, Oregon, "The employers also succeeded in getting unionized workers to accept lower wage increases than in the past." Mark Husson, a food and drug analyst for Merrill Lynch Global Securities, described Wal-Mart's low worker costs as its main competitive advantage. In the fall of 2003, during a grocery workers' strike in Southern California, Husson told a reporter for the *Contra Costa [CA] Times*: "Wal-Mart is soon going to be the lowest common denominator in the food business, and everyone has to move towards that level."

During similar union negotiations in 2003 in St. Louis, three large grocery stores, Schnucks, Dierbergs and Shop 'n Save, asked for concessions from their 10,000 workers. The grocery stores wanted to "level the playing field" with discount stores like Wal-Mart by cutting back on health care costs. Wal-Mart has eight supercenters in the St. Louis area, and their over-saturation has forced other grocery stores to look for ways to lower their labor costs. "We are not using Wal-Mart as a scare tactic," explained a spokesman for Shop 'n Save. "We need to find a more effective way to communicate to our associates that it is a problem and that we are scared. The three of us [grocery stores] are scared that one of us is not going to be in business at some point in the future. We don't know when. Is it tomorrow? No. Is it a year from now? No. But at some point, one of us is not going to be here, because there is not enough business for all of us and Wal-Mart."

Workers were asked to pay for a larger share of the cost of their medical bills, with higher deductibles and co-payments. The union was also asked to accept lower wage increases in the future. "The wage increases are a joke," one dairy manager with 29 years work experience told the *St. Louis Post-Dispatch*. "How do they expect people to live? We can't earn enough to keep pace with what's going on in the world."

In October 2003, unionized grocery workers were locked out of their stores at Von's, Albertson's and Ralph's in southern California. According to the *Irvine [CA] Progressive*, the grocery stores were seeking to create a two-tier benefit system, in which current workers would get some of their current benefits, and new hires would get no benefits and lower wages. Over time, these stores would become "Wal-Martized." The striking workers claimed that these three grocers have plans to phase-in non-union stores, to phase out butchers and food clerks. One union worker told the paper, "We're told Wal-Mart sends their employees to get food stamps because they don't pay them enough to afford food. And this is what Albertson's aspires to become?"

In fact, California Assemblywoman Sally Lieber, D-San Jose, charged in July 2003 that Wal-Mart was instructing its workers how to take advantage of government welfare programs. Lieber showed the media Wal-Mart employee hand-outs telling workers how to use an employment verification service when applying for government aid, like Medicaid, food stamps and temporary assistance to needy families. Lieber said this was proof that Wal-Mart was expecting the state and federal government to make up for what she described as "poverty" level wages and benefits.

The Wal-Mart handout to its employees explained how they could use an employment verification service if an "associate" wanted to rent an apartment or borrow money. The landlord or bank could call a special number to verify that the workers was employed at Wal-Mart. Wal-Mart also explained in the flier that its workers can use the same service when applying for government assistance. The handout explained how a social service caseworker could check an employee's income to determine whether they would qualify for government assistance.

Assemblywoman Lieber told the *Contra Costa Times* that California was going through the "worst budget crisis since the Great Depression," and added, "In that context, we can't keep large, wealthy corporations on the dole."

Besides employee wages, the other key cost factor that Wal-Mart has sought to restrain is health insurance. Although Wal-Mart describes its health coverage as "a very affordable plan," the company's workers have to contend with monthly premiums, deductibles, and a one-third co-pay for services. The UFCW claims that Wal-Mart spends 40% less than all U.S. corporations on health benefits for each of its employees. According to a report by Mercer Human Resource Consulting, Wal-Mart spends less money on health care coverage than retailers and non-competitors. Wal-Mart spent an average of $3,500 per worker for health benefits in 2002. That's compared with $5,646 per worker for all employers and $4,834 per worker in the wholesale and retail industries.

Thousands of Wal-Mart workers don't buy the health plan because they can't afford it. "Most doctors in this area will be quick to ask you for a second insurance to cover your bills," one Wal-Mart worker wrote me. "It took me two and a half years to pay my doctor bill. Wal-Mart paid some of my bill: twenty bucks. I footed the rest of my $2,500 bill."

When Wal-Mart announced it was changing its health insurance company in October of 2003 from Cigna to Blue Cross Blue Shield, the company admitted that only half of its employees get their health insurance from Wal-Mart. They told the *Arkansas Democrat-Gazette* that another 40% of their workers "are covered under other health insurance" — but not paid for by Wal-Mart. This translates into nearly 630,000 workers on the Wal-Mart payroll with no health insurance.

Wal-Mart also makes its part-time workers, called "off-peak" associates, wait two years before becoming eligible for the health plan, and full-time workers have to wait six months to become eligible. High employee turnover means that many workers simply don't work long enough at Wal-Mart to get health insurance coverage, thereby working most of their time at the company uncovered.

In addition to the waiting period for health care eligibility, another factor holding down insurance enrollment at Wal-Mart is the out-of-pocket costs to the employee. According to research by the UFCW released in September 2003, the Wal-Mart health insurance deductible can range as high as $1,000 — three times the normal corporate health plan. As of January 1, 2004, a Wal-Mart employee seeking family coverage for health insurance pays $3,445 a year in premiums alone, plus a $350 deductible. A full-time worker at Wal-Mart with 28 hours a week on the clock, working at $7.50 an hour, would pay 35% of their gross paycheck on health premiums and deductibles, before collecting even one penny in benefits. Many employees just can't set aside the money to pay for the company's health care plan. For part-time workers, even if they stay on the job long enough to qualify for the plan, the premiums are just not affordable.

Just before Halloween 2003, the AFL-CIO released a report critical of Wal-Mart wages and health benefits. The study said that health care benefits at Wal-Mart may be unaffordable to families relying on an $8-an-hour breadwinner. "Less than half the employees of this company have health coverage," the AFL-CIO reported.

A Wal-Mart spokesman said that the company's health insurance plan requires the employee to pay a lot out of their own pocket because the coverage is only meant to help with very large bills. "Our argument is that our coverage is intentionally planned for those kinds of catastrophic issues," Bob McAdam, Wal-Mart's vice president of government relations, told the *Contra Costa Times*. McAdam said 40% of his workers get benefits from other sources including parents or spouses.

Another Wal-Mart spokesperson, Mia Masten, was even more blunt. "We are very upfront about the fact that many of our jobs are not designed to fully support a family," she told the *Woonsocket (RI) Call*.

## Sub-count B:  Illegal Workers

As if subsistence wages and fringe benefits were not criticism enough of the plantation-like environment at Wal-Mart, the company

13

had to weather yet another labor-related problem in October 2003: illegal workers. Wal-Mart received a blast of negative media exposure over a sting operation conducted by the federal government's Department of Homeland Security. Federal agents were all over Wal-Mart corporate headquarters, and stores in 21 states, as the government arrested 300 cleaning workers from Mexico and Eastern European nations on immigration charges. The sting gathered up workers at 60 Wal-Marts across the country.

Even more damaging to Wal-Mart's carefully cultivated corporate image, U.S. officials revealed that some Wal-Mart executives in Bentonville, Arkansas knew all about the use of illegal workers. It turns out that Wal-Mart had been cited before for using illegal workers not just to clean their stores — but to build them as well.

In a clear display of government sarcasm, the Wal-Mart investigation was called "Operation Rollback," a reference to the retailer's advertising focus on "rolling back" prices. News reports said the government had tape recordings of Wal-Mart executives, and had even searched their corporate beehive in Bentonville. It was suggested that federal grand jury subpoenas had been issued for unnamed Wal-Mart executives to testify. The federal officials investigating the case were quoted as saying the giant retailer had shown a "reckless disregard" for U.S. immigration laws, hiring some contractors who had already been convicted of felony violations. Wal-Mart did not exactly try to deny the charges in their carefully worded reply to reporters. "We have seen no evidence from the INS that anyone from Wal-Mart was involved in this," company spokeswoman Sharon Weber told *The Associated Press*.

A Wal-Mart spokesman sought to unload the burden by saying the cleaning crews were hired by "third-party contractors," who were supposed to "use legal workers." The company said it used "hundreds" of outside contractors. Roughly one-third of Wal-Mart's stores use outside cleaning services. But the image of the Department of Homeland Security's Bureau of Immigration and Customs Enforcement poring through Wal-Mart files in 21 states was a setback for the company's public relations machine.

If Wal-Mart is found guilty of knowingly hiring illegal workers, the company could face up to $10,000 in fines per person — which is a few seconds worth of sales to Wal-Mart. Although the public relations damage would be costly to the company, the real cost came to the workers with mops and buckets who were cleaned out of the Wal-Mart stores.

Illegal aliens cleaning the floors at Wal-Mart were paid in cash and didn't know the name of their employer. In return for their decision to work at Wal-Mart, they ended up paying the highest price: deportation.

According to an article in the October 25, 2003 *Star-Ledger (NJ)*, at the end of each week, a paycheck for the illegal cleaning crew would appear beneath the battery charger in the maintenance closet. The cleaning crew chief would then cash the check and divvy it up among his or her crew, in cash.

The newspaper described these aliens' chain of command as "a shadowy multi-tiered management system in which groups of illegal immigrants work for bosses they've never met and for companies some cannot name." The father of two cleaning crew workers called the illegal status of these workers "really just an out-loud secret."

The illegals appear to have been organized as subcontractors for the cleaning companies, who in turn contracted directly with Wal-Mart. The workers were hired into crews of half a dozen people per store. When the last customers left, the crews would come in and clean. The workers had few days off, were paid around $6 or $6.50 per hour, and had no health insurance or other fringe benefits. It appears unlikely, therefore, that any Social Security taxes or federal/state income taxes were withheld from their pay. Their relationship appears to be strictly on a cash basis with the crew boss.

One crew chief responsible for cleaning the Piscataway, New Jersey Wal-Mart recruited his Mexican workers from a local laundromat and train station. The crew boss told reporters that after working for six days, a check was left in the store's maintenance closet. The crew boss would cash it, take off the top his share of $350, and then pass the rest of the payment to his crew in cash. The arrested workers told officials they had met their supervisors face-to-face, but never were given their names. "If you asked me the name of the company, I wouldn't know," one crew boss told the *Star-Ledger*. "If you asked me what my boss looks like, I wouldn't know. I'm not playing with you." These workers now face a deportation hearing. They may be kicked out of the country without ever knowing whom their employer was. All this talk of secrecy and deportation made Wal-Mart's use of illegals sound like a terrorist cell.

The cleaning crew scandal was not the first time that Wal-Mart had been caught in a compromising use of illegal workers. Wal-Mart's close encounter in 2003 with illegal aliens was a flashback to a similar incident in Lake Charles, Louisiana two years earlier. Neighbors of the Super Wal-Mart under construction on Nelson Road asked the Border Patrol to check if the workers building the store were illegal. The Patrol first rounded up several of the workers for interviews. While returning one legal worker back to the job site, several other workers fled from the scene when they saw the Border Patrol car. Agents pursued them through the neighborhood. Along with Sheriff's Deputies, the Immigration and Naturalization Service arrested 29 illegal aliens working on the Wal-Mart. The Wal-Mexicans were carrying counterfeit Social Security cards, doctored immigration cards, and phony driver's licenses. "This is odd," a Border Patrol agent said. "Usually just a handful will have fake documents, but for all to have counterfeit cards — it's a little strange." Most of the workers had been sleeping at the nearby Inn on the Bayou, and were reportedly working for two construction companies.

Several months later, members of the International Brotherhood of Electrical Workers, Local 861, complained to the Lake Charles City Council that no local contractors, electricians, or vendors were being used to build the Nelson Road store. The union asked the city officials to look into the possibility of revoking the building permits of any company found to be using illegal aliens. One member of the Council suggested that the city withdraw its support of Wal-Mart's state enterprise zone application, which returns a part of state sales tax to the retailer. One resident told the newspaper that he was at a hearing between city officials and Wal-Mart in March 2001 when a Wal-Mart representative told a City Councilor "that if he ever brought up the subject of illegal aliens again, (he) should not ever ask him to bring another Wal-Mart into this city."

Whether it was the sweatshop labor that made Kathie Lee Gifford clothes, or the Mexicans who built their stores, or the illegals who cleaned the floors, Wal-Mart always had the protection of plausible deniability. Their stock line was that these workers "do not work for us" and they are the responsibility of hundreds of "subcontractors" or "vendors." Because Wal-Mart owns none of its manufacturing operations, it can say, from an arms-length distance, as David Glass once told NBC's Dateline: "Yeah, there are tragic things that happen all over the world."

Wal-Mart exists in this buffer zone, surrounded by deniability, while the people who clean up after their shoppers, who sew their private label clothing, and even those who work on their own sales floor — are just units of production.

## Sub-count C: Employee Lawsuits

It is inevitable that with 1.4 million workers, there are bound to be some people on the Wal-Mart payroll who do not love their job. Not all Wal-Mart workers are smiling along with the yellow Mr. Smiley buttons placed prominently on their work vests. *The New York Times* on June 25, 2002 carried an article about lawsuits filed by Wal-Mart "associates" in 28 states. The litigation asserted that Wal-Mart had a policy of denying overtime pay and forcing its own people to work off the clock. One newspaper editorial writer called this "stealing from the employees."

The lawsuits brought by employees charge that the company cheated its own workers out of millions of dollars a year in pay they never received. Wal-Mart claims that "off the clock" work is "infrequent and isolated," but in 2000, Wal-Mart had to pay $50 million to settle a lawsuit that involved 69,000 workers in Colorado who had worked off the clock. In Texas, *The New York Times* reported that 200,000 "associates" charged Wal-Mart with underpaying them as much as $150 million over four year's time. In other states, workers complained of being routinely locked in the store at night to finish cleaning up their departments, sometimes without any staff present having a key to get out. Workers didn't complain, because they were afraid of getting fired. Employees have told me that every Wal-Mart store has a payroll "budget" based on sales. In addition, Wal-Mart's computer allows managers to edit the times that punches are recorded on employees' time cards. *The New York Times* referred to this practice as "the creative timecard."

The alleged "time theft" by Wal-Mart against its own workers might not amount to a hill of timecards for an individual worker — but the accumulated effect could be dramatic. Russell Lloyd, an attorney who is representing 21 plaintiffs in wage violation lawsuits against Wal-Mart, told the *NOW with Bill Moyers* show in November 2002 that workers lost "a little here, a little there" and that most off the clock claims would not come to more than a few thousand dollars per employee. But Lloyd suggested that the total value of these uncompensated hours could represent huge savings to Wal-Mart's cost of doing business. Just one hour per worker of unpaid overtime in one store with 250 workers would mean more than 13,050 hours per year. Assuming 3,351 Wal-Mart stores in 2003, the savings to the company are super-sized. Using a conservative figure of $7.00 per hour, Wal-Mart could save $306 million in unpaid wages a year — not counting any fringe benefits.

Wal-Mart protests that such time theft from its workers is against company policy, but one Wal-Mart worker told *NOW*: "Well, the manager would say, do me a favor, you know, I'll try to find somebody to work over there, and then it would never happen. I would stay there up to four or five hours off the clock and they would never find anybody there to take my place. And I knew that, if I were to leave, I wouldn't have a job when I got back."

Not only did former Wal-Mart assistant managers confirm this practice to *NOW*, but a payroll clerk as well, who said management ordered her to alter the time records of employees in the Louisiana Wal-Mart store where she worked. "It's Wal-Mart's system that does this," the payroll clerk admitted. "People like me who went in there and did exactly what they told me to do."

Over the years, Wal-Mart has also had serious challenges to its workforce policies from its women workers. *Fortune* magazine has called Wal-Mart "America's Most Admired Retailer." But the company is also America's Most Sued Retailer, according to walmartlitigation.com, which is maintained by an attorney who has handled lawsuits against Wal-Mart. The company reported nearly 5,000 lawsuits filed against it in 2001, a rate of roughly one lawsuit every two hours. Jury verdicts are reached at a rate of six per day. This makes Wal-Mart the second most sued entity in the U.S., behind only the federal government, according to *USA Today*. In October 2003, Wal-Mart told the *Associated Press* that the retailer had 6,949 active lawsuits against it.

According to Wal-Mart's own filing with the Securities and Exchange Commission, "The company is involved in a number of legal proceedings, including anti-trust, consumer employment, tort, and other litigation." Wal-Mart admits that if they lose these lawsuits, it "may result in liability material to the Company's consolidated financial statements." In other words, if Wal-Mart loses big class action lawsuits, it could have a serious impact on the company's profits. The damage to the corporation's good will could resonate for years.

One of the lawsuits most threatening to the company's bottom line is *Dukes v. Wal-Mart Stores, Inc.* As Wal-Mart describes it to stockholders in its 2004 Annual Report, the *Dukes* case, which could involve between 700,000 and 1.5 million of its female employees, "alleges that the company has a pattern and practice of discriminating against women in promotions, pay, training and job assignments. The complaint seeks, among other things, injunctive relief, compensatory damages — including front pay and back pay, punitive damages, and attorney fees."

In April 2003, in San Francisco U.S. District Court, lawyers for the female employees filed a motion for class action certification. The motion asked the judge to allow the case to go to trial on behalf of all women who have worked at Wal-Mart stores in America since December 26, 1998. This would make the case the largest employment discrimination case ever filed — bigger than a similar case at Home Depot several years ago that resulted in a payment by Home Depot in excess of $100 million. The motion filed in *Dukes* named 110 women who worked at 184 Wal-Mart stores. It charged that two out of three (65%) of Wal-Mart's sales force are women, but only one in three (33%) of store management positions are held by women, and less than one in seven (14%) store manager positions are women. The plaintiffs claim that women managers earn only 85% of the pay earned by males in the same positions. The motion claims that Wal-Mart payroll data shows that women are paid less than men are with the same seniority, even though women have higher performance ratings and less turnover. According to an April 2003 *Business Wire* report, Wal-Mart's court filings suggest the company is "behind the rest of the world" in promoting women to management positions. "Women are treated as second class employees at Wal-Marts from Florida to Alaska," said a spokesman for The Impact Fund, which is coordinating the lawsuit. "This is not just an isolated or local problem. Wal-Mart has known about this for years and has refused to act."

The lawsuit charges that senior management at Wal-Mart used demeaning stereotypes of women, and that female managers were forced to go to Hooters sports bars and strip clubs for office outings. One male manager in Texas told a female employee that women have to be "bitches" to survive Wal-Mart management. Another manager in California told a woman she should "doll up" to get promoted. Ramona Scott, a female personnel manager in Pinellas Park, Florida was told by her manager, "Men are here to make a career and women aren't. Retail is for housewives who just need to earn extra money." Scott claims that Wal-Mart segregated its workers along gender lines — putting women at the cash registers and men in the electronics and sporting goods sections. Scott said she and Wal-Mart parted ways in 1998, when a male manager told her that to get along with him, "I needed to behave like his wife."

Wal-Mart tried to get the lawsuit moved from San Francisco to Arkansas. The court rejected that motion. Because of its treatment of female workers, Wal-Mart was designated by the National Organization for Women (NOW) as a "Merchant of Shame" — a stark contrast to the company's promotion of itself as *Fortune* magazine's "Most Admired Retailer."

Some Wal-Mart workers claim they live in a world of constant harassment and intimidation. Carolyn Thiebes, who worked at a Wal-Mart store in Salem, Oregon, testified in a wage and hours lawsuit in November 2002, that the happy Mr. Smiley image was not at all her experience working at Wal-Mart.

Thiebes testified that when her department failed to meet company expectations, her boss would single out the personnel manager by hanging a red bandana near her door for a month for all co-workers to see. The Wal-Mart managers also had a trophy, which was molded in the shape of a horse's hindquarters, and was called "the horse's ass award."

"It was humiliating," Thiebes told the court. "That trophy was given so many times — anytime a department failed."

Thiebes said she and her co-workers had to stay after their shifts, working off the clock to get their jobs done. This happened so often, these workers became known as "the Over 40 club." These workers would routinely clock out, then return to their workstations to complete the day's assignments. One Wal-Mart lawn and garden department manager said he worked unpaid hours out of fear for what would happen if he didn't. "Because it's such a small community, jobs aren't that good there. You held on to your job. I feared losing my job. I feared getting fired."

Wal-Mart tells its employees: "Our people make the difference." Yet the company seems disinterested in the plight of its own people at a time when they need company support the most.

Tom Davis died in 1992 at the age of 40 while operating a forklift as an employee of a Sam's Club in Oakwood Village, Ohio. For his family, Davis' death was just the beginning — not the end — of their misfortunes.

While moving produce from a truck to the loading dock, the truck moved away from the dock. The forklift and its contents fell on Davis and crushed him. During the lawsuit filed by his widow, Davis' attorneys learned of a Wal-Mart memo written eight months before Davis' death describing similar dock accidents, and outlining procedures for preventing reoccurrence. The memo said that Sam's Club had had several incidents where trucks "prematurely pulled away from our dock while an associate and/or lift equipment was still on the truck." At the trial, Wal-Mart did not admit this document existed—until Davis' lawyers indicated they already had it.

Wal-Mart claimed they kept no accident records. After deliberating for 40 minutes, jurors in the 1995 case awarded Davis' widow $2 million. Davis' lawyers also uncovered the fact in the company's lawyer's diary that Wal-Mart had, in fact, detailed reports of many similar dock accidents that led to the issuance of the memo, even though the company claimed in court that it had no such records.

Two years later, Davis' widow sued Wal-Mart again for suppressing documents, thereby hindering her from seeking punitive damages. The second case went to the Ohio Supreme Court, which chided Wal-Mart for playing "hide the thimble" with key evidence. The court ordered Wal-Mart to produce files back to 1990 of all the decisions in which it was charged with holding back key evidence during the "discovery" phase of investigations.

Wal-Mart then settled the lawsuit with Davis' widow, so the documents never were released. Davis' attorney, William Greene, wrote to Wal-Mart's lawyer: "It is one thing to kill your own employee recklessly and 'intentionally,' but quite another thing to cheat his widow..."

Wal-Mart's deal with Davis' widow to end her second lawsuit is confidential. The amount of the financial award was never made public. Ironically, the Davis family was willing to settle at one point for $250,000, but Wal-Mart's ten year battle with Davis' family ended up costing them at least ten times that amount.

Wal-Mart has also fought with its own workers over stolen merchandise. Veteran workers at Wal-Mart have been fired for eating taco chips from an open bag in the employee's lounge. This is strange, since Helen Walton, Sam's widow, has admitted that in the early days of her husband's career, she used to stop by the Walton Five and Dime, take whatever she wanted from the shelves, and walk out without paying for it. "If I needed something, I just got it and took it home with me." Once the Wal-Mart stores were in operation, Helen Walton said it was a "real shock" when she had to start paying for things.

Wal-Mart employees have had to pay for things, too. I have often heard from employees who complained that the company tried to blame them for some theft from the company — sometimes as a way to terminate the employee.

In February 2002, a federal jury in Burlington, Vermont ruled that Kristy Myers, a Wal-Mart employee, should be given $26,473 by her employer in back wages and damages.

Myers worked for Wal-Mart in the pharmacy department. She sued the company in 2000, saying that she was frequently forced to work overtime without pay. While she was "off the clock," she had to put up in-store displays, go around town checking the price of competitors' drugs, and deliver gifts to doctors' offices to encourage prescription referrals.

In court, Myers testified that on her own time she had to take damaged goods to a local health program. "I would give them damaged goods, things we could not return and get our money back for."

But not being paid for the hours she worked was just a small part of what happened to Kristy Myers while she wore a Wal-Mart vest. Myers was also held against her will in the store. She told jurors that on one of her vacation days, she was working on a display when Wal-Mart's "shoplifting" (they call it "loss prevention") specialist took her into a backroom in the store and interrogated her for three hours.

Wal-Mart accused her of stealing $20,000 in merchandise — a figure the company later adjusted to $2,000. The company told Myers that if she didn't confess, she would spend the night in jail while Wal-Mart went to her home and conducted a search for stolen goods. "It was the worst experience in my whole life," Myers told the *Burlington Free Press*.

Scared and under stress, Myers signed a confession and was fired. For most of the items "stolen," Myers had kept receipts.

Wal-Mart said that Myers had confessed to the theft. But the jury didn't believe any of it. They found Kristy Myers' testimony more credible than Wal-Mart's — and they ruled in her favor. "We are disappointed in the jury verdict," a Wal-Mart spokesman said.

## Sub-count D: Unjust Enrichment

The retailer's hold over its workers even extends beyond death. One of the more bizarre relationships that Wal-Mart establishes with its workers is an insurance product called company-owned life insurance (COLI).

The image that Wal-Mart likes to project of its associates is that of one big, loving family. "We're all members of a family that really cares — the Wal-Mart family," Rob Walton, the Chairman of Wal-Mart Stores, says in his father's autobiography. When Rob was a child, he worked in his Dad's stores, sweeping floors, carrying boxes, and "even running the ice cream machine." "I remember feeling," he says, "that all the associates in the store were part of the family." But sometimes Wal-Mart extends that "part of the family" concept beyond its normal bounds.

Douglas Sims was part of the Wal-Mart family. Sims died in 1998 of a heart attack. His wife, Jane, had little time to prepare for his sudden death.

Fortunately, Jane Sims found out that her husband had a life insurance policy from his employer, Wal-Mart. Unfortunately, the life insurance left Jane Sims no money at all. Everything — roughly $64,000 — went to Wal-Mart.

Doug Sims had worked at a Wal-Mart distribution center in Plainview, Texas for 11 years. His wife had no idea that Wal-Mart was named the beneficiary of his life insurance policy. When she learned of the "secret" policy several years later, she filed a lawsuit against the company.

This form of life insurance is called company-owned life insurance, or COLI. Such policies are also sometimes referred to as "dead peasant" insurance. To take out the policy, Wal-Mart borrowed money from insurance companies like Hartford Life or AIG Life to pay for the premiums, and then wrote off the cost of those premiums on their federal taxes as a cost of doing business. In this way, the U.S. taxpayer has been subsidizing Wal-Mart to profit from the death of its own workers.

In Texas, only people with an "insurable interest" can take out a life insurance policy on another person. That is usually defined as their spouse or other family member, a creditor, or "one having a reasonable expectation of pecuniary benefit or advantage from the continued life of another." Even though company-owned policies are illegal in Texas, Wal-Mart argued that the policies were signed in Georgia, where state law says nothing on the subject.

Apparently, the Wal-Mart practice of taking out life insurance on its own workers dates back to the mid-1990's. The company offered its employees a "special" death benefit offer worth $5,000 — but there was an underlying related policy that was worth far more to Wal-Mart. Some

23

employees never knew that beneath the surface of the death benefit plan, the company was the real beneficiary.

In its 2003 Annual Report to stockholders, Wal-Mart admitted that it was a defendant "in three putative class action lawsuits in Texas, one in New Hampshire, and one in Oklahoma" over these dead peasant policies. The lawsuits charge that Wal-Mart "lacks an insurable interest in the lives [of its workers]...who were the insureds under the policies, and seeks to recover the proceeds of the policies under theories of unjust enrichment and constructive trust." Jane Sims argued that Wal-Mart unjustly enriched itself off the death of her husband.

In August 2002, Wal-Mart tried to get the Sims case thrown out in a summary judgment, but the Texas court ruled in favor of Jane Sims. Wal-Mart then appealed that decision to the Fifth Circuit Court of Appeals. Five years after her husband's death, Jane Sims still had not collected one penny from his life insurance. " I never dreamed they could profit from my husband's death," Sims told the *Houston Chronicle*. A spokesman for Wal-Mart told the same newspaper: "The company feels it acted properly and legally in doing this."

In January 2004 the Sims case was finally settled out of court. The 5th U.S. Circuit Court of Appeals ruled that Wal-Mart "unlawfully took funds, that, under Texas law, rightfully belonged" to the relatives of the dead Wal-Mart workers. According to the *Associated Press*, Houston Attorney Mike Myers, who represented the plaintiffs, said, "A large percentage of the population doesn't approve of the morality or the ethics of this type of conduct. My client's reaction, when they found out, was stunned and disbelief, turning to frustration and anger."

Wal-Mart settled the Houston case hours before the court ruling. The financial terms of the deal were not disclosed, but the company said it would affect relatives of as many as 500 dead Wal-Mart workers in Texas alone. A Wal-Mart spokesman said the company was happy the case was now over, and said the retailer lost $100 million on these policies, and stopped issuing them three years ago, after court decisions stripped the policies of any tax benefits.

Wal-Mart is suing the two insurance companies that wrote these policies, AIG and Hartford Life, trying to force the insurance companies to pay Wal-Mart for their losses on the policies, including the Texas settlement. Ten years ago, Wal-Mart created a trust that named itself the beneficiary on policies written on 350,000 employees.

Jane Sims was quoted as saying, "They used my husband. It's wrong. Morally wrong."

## Sub-count E: Sweatshop Labor

Over the years, Wal-Mart has also found it proper and legal to use child labor to produce its merchandise. The modern retail corporation does not own production factories. It makes nothing. The thousands of factories that make Wal-Mart products — many of them now located in foreign countries — employ workers that technically have no corporate ties to the company other than an order form. Although labor rights groups have tried to get retailers to monitor their vendors to meet a code of conduct, the abuse of workers in sweatshops is seen as an unfortunate but distant problem. In this way, the company is in a position of plausible deniability. Wal-Mart can disassociate itself from the people and places where its products are made, as if the products on its shelves were immaculately conceived. More than a decade ago, this disconnect between buyer and producer was put in stark relief by the head of America's largest retailer.

David Glass, CEO of the fastest-growing retailer in the world, was interviewed in 1992 by NBC's *Dateline* show. Glass' stony, angular face showed no emotional response. Brian Ross, a reporter with *Dateline*, was seated next to a TV monitor that faced Glass.

Glass, the carefully chosen successor to Sam Walton, was shown shots of the inside of the Sharaka clothing factory in Bangladesh. Ross described for Glass a "factory full of children" — a workplace that two years prior was the site of a deadly fire that killed 25 workers, many of them children. The factory was surrounded by armed guards and barbed wire.

Ross: The children who work in this plant are locked in until all hours of the night, until they finish the day's production.
Glass: Yeah, there are tragic things that happen all over the world.

Glass stares back at Ross, his face empty of expression.

Ross: That's all you want to say about it?
Glass: I don't know what else I would say about it.

At this point, Don Shinkle, a Wal-Mart vice president, stepped forward and stopped the interview, and Glass was led out of the room.

Two weeks later, Wal-Mart called *Dateline* back and asked to continue the interview.

Glass started off the continuation of the interview by claiming that Wal-Mart had sent someone to Bangladesh to check out the Sharaka factory, and that no evidence of child labor was discovered.

> Ross: Your man was there and he saw no children working in that factory?
> Glass: No.
> Ross: Or any of the other factories?
> Glass: Children — you and I might, perhaps define children differently. In Bangladesh...
> Ross: Should a 12-year-old girl be in school or making clothes for Wal-Mart? Anywhere in the world?
> Glass: No, we — a 12-year-old girl should not.
> Ross: But they are. We saw them.
> Glass: Well, we have not been able to substantiate that.

The interview continued to slide downhill. Glass continued to doubt the authenticity of the video accounts of Wal-Mart sweatshop labor.

> Glass: The — the picture — the-the-the pictures you showed me mean nothing to me. I'm — I'm not sure where they were or who they were, you know. Could have been of anything. I'm not sure.
> Ross: I'm telling you, they're not of anything, they're of the Sharaka factory, of children making Wal-Mart clothing.
> Glass: Well, I'm — I'm comfortable with what we have done.

# Count 3:
# Exploiting Your Suppliers

*"When you drive the cost of a product down, you really can't deliver the high-quality product like we have."*
—James Weir, CEO, Simplicity Manufacturing, October, 2003

Wal-Mart's reputation rests on its low prices. But sometimes there are side effects to these low prices that consumers don't normally think about. They include:

- Loss of American jobs to foreign competitors
- Lower quality of products on Wal-Mart shelves because of the pressure on manufacturers to cut costs
- Destruction of the value of brand names as Wal-Mart tries to fool its shoppers with lower priced rip-offs of familiar products.

Here are some examples of how Wal-Mart can harm its suppliers:

Simplicity Manufacturing makes lawn mowers. They decided in 2002 to stop selling to Wal-Mart. The CEO told *Business Week* magazine that the decision to cut off relations with Wal-Mart was because the retailer made it impossible for them to put a quality mower on the market. "Wal-Mart really is about driving the cost of a product down."

In the fall of 2003, a Vero Beach, Florida company that sold candles and office chairs to Wal-Mart sued the retailer for $1 billion, charging that company managers tried to steal away his business. Owner Jeffrey Saull says that a Wal-Mart manager and buyer tried to get Saull's candle supplier to drop his company and force it into bankruptcy. "Years of hard work have been uprooted," Saull told the *Associated Press*. "This is not a vision of how good, hard-working companies should behave. I'm all about the small guy, and I'm about to take on this giant."

In April 1999, *Inc.* magazine ran a feature story about GTO, a Florida vendor that made automatic gate openers for Wal-Mart. "Seasoned vendors to the so-called big boxes know that dealing with them requires a constant series of compromises and accommodations," *Inc.* reported. "They believe such slights and injustices are costs of doing business, not the stuff of litigation." But GTO eventually sued Wal-Mart for breach of contract in 1996 for:

- sending the manufacturer back "defective" products that were not defective;
- taking cash discounts off its invoices even when Wal-Mart didn't pay on a timely basis; and
- seeking other unauthorized credits.

At one point, GTO claimed Wal-Mart owed them nearly $45,000 in "invalid" returns. Wal-Mart had also mistakenly sent the company items that GTO didn't even make, like diapers, car winches, and bicycle chains. GTO sued Wal-Mart for more than half a million dollars, and in a court settlement received nearly the full award — for a case that should never have happened in the first place.

According to an article in *The New York Times* on October 22, 2000: "Whether Wal-Mart's demands [on its vendors] cross the line from the obsessive to the crushing is a subject of hot debate among suppliers. But Wal-Mart's purchasing power is so great that none of its trading partners were willing to go on the record saying negative things about it."

This is not surprising, since Wal-Mart purchases a considerable percentage share of many producers' output. 28% of Dial soap is sold at Wal-Mart. 23% of Clorox. 22% of Revlon products. 17% of Proctor & Gamble. 12% of Kraft Foods. 12% of General Mills. 12% of Kellogg. 10% of Sara Lee. The clout of this market share has put Wal-Mart in the position of dictating terms to the vendors, rather than the reverse.

I was doing a radio talk show from Madison, Wisconsin in the fall of 2002, when a caller phoned in:

"I work for a small manufacturer near here. I don't want to identify the company. We have a major contract with Wal-Mart. One day we sent them an order, and the payment comes back $13,000 short. So we called them up and said, 'What gives?' Wal-Mart says to us: 'We noticed on your billing terms that we have 45 days to make our payments to you. On our last three orders, we have been paying you before the 45 days were up. If we waited the full 45 days to pay you, we would have saved ourselves $13,000. So we are deducting that amount from this month's invoice."

At this point, the talk show host interrupted, "Oh, come on now. Did they really do that? You've got to be kidding." To which the caller replied, "I wish I was."

Wal-Mart's no-holds-barred reputation with vendors is legendary. As the predominant buyer in America, Wal-Mart has the leverage to dictate the terms of this relationship. Many of the venerable brand name consumer goods manufacturers in America have become dependent on Wal-Mart for their very survival. The power base today rests with the retailer — not the supplier. Whatever Wal-Mart wants, Wal-Mart gets — and the vendors find themselves reinvented to fit the specifications that Wal-Mart demands. To bring down prices to meet Wal-Mart goals means cutting costs, and cutting jobs.

Levi Strauss is a company that has had a dominant brand name for much of its 150-year history. The company faced one of its greatest challenges when Wal-Mart began selling its own "Faded Glory" brand of jeans. Wal-Mart sells more jeans than any retailer in America, and "Faded Glory" sales alone are nearly as large as Levi Strauss' sales. As sales at Levi Strauss faded, the company sat down with its rival producer — Wal-Mart — and negotiated a sales agreement that would get Levi jeans into Wal-Mart stores. But at a price.

It was not the premium, more expensive Levi Strauss jeans that went into thousands of Wal-Mart stores. It was a different product. Levi Strauss created a special Signature brand jean only available at Wal-Mart. Levi Strauss sales, which had become unzipped, began to rise again — thanks to Wal-Mart sales. Levi Strauss dedicated a number of management staff for the Wal-Mart account, but the impact on the factory worker was not as attractive. The company ripped the seams out of several production plants in North America, and moved the labor to Asia and South America. The Levi Strauss name is on the Wal-Mart jeans, but any difference in the quality of the jeans — or where it was fabricated — may be lost on the customer.

In January 2004 Levi Strauss announced that it was shutting

down its last American-based production plants in San Antonio, Texas, eliminating the jobs of 800 sewers and finishers. "We tried to do our best to maintain manufacturing in the United States," a Levi Strauss spokesman told the *Miami Herald*, "but we have to be competitive to survive as a company." At its high point, the San Antonio plants produced 4 million pairs of Levi's, and the workers made an average of $12 an hour.

"We're still an American brand," the company spokesman added, "but we're also a brand and a company whose products have been adopted by consumers around the world. We have to operate as a global company."

Levi Strauss gave its laid off workers $2,450 each, and severance pay of two weeks for every year worked at the company. Rosalinda Medina, who worked for Levi's in San Antonio for nearly 25 years, told a local radio station, "I am a little bit angry that [Levi Strauss] is going overseas. That's the only thing that bothers me, that we have to give up our jobs so they can get cheaper labor."

A similar scenario took place at Master Lock. Although the Master Lock company could never boast that it had a lock on market share in its industry, its parent company, MasterBrand Industries, had a recognizable brand name and a reliable product with good consumer acceptance. Master Lock was also synonymous with manufacturing in Milwaukee, Wisconsin, where the company had been operating since 1922.

What Master Lock could not keep under lock and key were the cheap foreign imports that began reaching U.S. shores in the 1990s. According to the November 14, 2003 issue of *Fast Company* magazine, foreign-made locks broke the hold Master Lock had on their product line. A former CEO of MasterBrand told *Fast Company*: "When the difference is $1, retailers like Wal-Mart would prefer to have the brand-name padlock or faucet or hammer. But as the spread becomes greater, when our padlock was $9, and the import was $6, then they can offer the consumer a real discount by carrying two lines. Ultimately, they may only carry one line."

Pressure to sell a cheaper lock to the likes of Wal-Mart forced Master Lock to search for cheaper labor, and have its products made off-shore. In 1997, the company announced that it would be importing more of its brand name goods from factories in Asia, and in that same year, Master Lock opened up its first factory in Nogales, Mexico.

Today, *Fast Company* estimates Master Lock makes roughly 90% of its locks in foreign factories and only 10% in Milwaukee. U.S. workers at the Master Lock facility fabricate parts that are sent to the larger factory in Nogales.

As many as 250 union workers lost their Master Lock jobs. The MasterBrand executive who negotiated with Wal-Mart said that the retailer argued that if Wal-Mart could buy a foreign-made lock that had similar quality to the Master Lock at a cheaper price, "Well, they can get their consumers a deal." The deal for Master Lock, however, meant laying off workers who made good wages with good health benefits. Master Lock changed its operations by outsourcing most of its products to third world countries and shrinking its American workforce — all to remain on Wal-Mart shelves.

A typical example of what has happened to American manufacturers comes from one of the signature products at Wal-Mart: underwear. Wal-Mart boasted in its 1996 Annual Report that it sold 1.13 pairs of underwear annually for every man, woman and child in America. One major Wal-Mart vendor is Fruit of the Loom, which is also the BVD brand. Fruit of the Loom and Wal-Mart are sewn together at the hip. Wal-Mart wants to sell cheap underwear to every American. The pressure is on Fruit of the Loom to deliver cheap underwear to its large customers, like Wal-Mart. To cut labor costs, Fruit of the Loom cut higher-wage U.S. jobs and shipped the work to apparel workers in third world countries. You and I got cheap underwear, the workers in Fruit of the Loom plants got pink slips.

In 1998, Fruit of the Loom announced that it was cutting 2,908 American jobs. The supplier said it had to tighten its belt in order to remain "a low-cost provider of quality family apparel." Wal-Mart is one of Fruit of the Loom's largest customers. Wal-Mart may be selling lots of cheap underwear, but that wasn't enough to save the jobs of workers in towns like Abbeville, Jeanerette and St. Martinville, Louisiana, or Jamestown and Campbellsville, Kentucky — the places where Fruit of the Loom factory jobs were cut.

Fruit of the Loom had 31,000 employees worldwide, but it moved many of its jobs overseas. According to a 1998 *Bloomberg News* report, Fruit of the Loom "began five years ago to move its more labor intensive operations, such as sewing, to Mexico, the Caribbean Islands, and other locations to save money."

A vendor's extreme makeover to please Wal-Mart is not an unusual tale. In July 2000 the *Akron Beacon Journal* carried a series on Wal-Mart's powerful chokehold over its manufacturers. The specific relationship between Rubbermaid and Wal-Mart illustrates some of the dangers to manufacturers of becoming dependent on one big customer.

Rubbermaid was one of the country's most ubiquitous makers of kitchenware. But by 1994, Rubbermaid was hitting rough financial times.

Within five years, Rubbermaid was bought out by a lesser-known manufacturer called the Newell Company. In those intervening years, Wal-Mart's pressure on Rubbermaid bounced the plastics company further into the red, and then into the arms of a competitor. A former Rubbermaid manager called this takeover "a sad story," and the story line is that Wal-Mart did Rubbermaid in.

In the mid-1990s, Rubbermaid was dealing with skyrocketing prices for resin, a key ingredient in its plastic products. In fact, the company lost $250 million in 1995 due to resin price hikes. When Rubbermaid tried to pass a higher price for its products on to Wal-Mart, the retailer warned that if prices rose, Rubbermaid products would be dropped. At the time, Wal-Mart represented as much as 20% of Rubbermaid's business. Rubbermaid executives told the *Beacon Journal* that Wal-Mart's selling of Rubbermaid products as loss leaders also hurt the supplier, because other stores wanted Rubbermaid to lower its prices for them as well. "They backed us into a corner," one Rubbermaid manager admitted. "We couldn't recoup our product development costs before they'd slash prices. That led to less innovation."

When Rubbermaid raised the prices of some of its toys to Wal-Mart, the retailer dropped the Rubbermaid toys, and dropped its kitchen products also, going with another company "adept at making Rubbermaid look-alikes at a lower cost." In 1995, Rubbermaid earnings plunged by 30%.

Wal-Mart also insisted that Rubbermaid get its products to Wal-Mart within 2 days of being ordered. If it didn't, it was fined for each dollar Wal-Mart said it lost, and was required to buy back unsold wares. Even further, Wal-Mart dictated to Rubbermaid what types of products it should make, and how it should make them. The former Rubbermaid manager said Wal-Mart "squeezed too hard."

In 1998, the troubled Rubbermaid was vulnerable to takeover, and the Newell company was there to capitalize on the opportunity. Once the company assumed control of Rubbermaid, Newell products started to reappear on Wal-Mart shelves — ostensibly because Newell company management agreed to do things "the Wal-Mart way." *Executive Intelligence Review* magazine, in a November 2003 article, claimed that Joseph Galli, the CEO of Newell Rubbermaid, had a series of meetings with Wal-Mart management in 2001 regarding what product line Rubbermaid should offer, and what the price of those items should be. After that meeting, Rubbermaid shut down 69 of its 400 factories and gave pink slips to some 11,000 employees. The magazine quotes a research director at Associated Trust & Company as saying that Galli had to "shift about 50% of production to low-cost countries, which meant more factory closures, and more laid off workers."

The *Beacon Journal* article suggests that Rubbermaid took a fall because they stood up to Wal-Mart demands. The Wooster, Ohio firm's fall was due, in part, to Wal-Mart's decision to pull Rubbermaid products from its shelves. Even a plastics company proved to be unable to bounce back from such an impact. The executives at Rubbermaid who defied Wal-Mart were replaced by more pliable managers when Newell took over production.

The impact of Wal-Mart power-brokering can affect a company with sudden and disastrous impacts. In Tulsa, Oklahoma, the ADDvantage Media Group watched a supplier's dream relationship with Wal-Mart turn into a lawsuit. ADDvantage marketed a solar-powered shopper's calculator mounted on a shopping cart. It allowed advertising displays to be inserted on the calculator. In 1993 and 1994, ADDvantage entered into contracts with Wal-Mart to install its calculators in certain Wal-Mart stores. When those contracts were not implemented, the company sued Wal-Mart for breach of contract. They reached a settlement in 1995 for a new contract to install calculators in all Wal-Mart supercenters. The calculator deal added up to some big numbers: $23.5 million in revenue for ADDvantage. As of the end of March 1998, ADDvantage had installed shopper's calculators in 336 Wal-Mart supercenters.

In 1997 the company submitted a proposal for a new contract with Wal-Mart to go beyond the $23.5 million level. But in the spring of 1998, Wal-Mart reversed direction, and told ADDvantage it would not enter into a new agreement or extend the old one. ADDvantage decided to sue Wal-Mart again, this time charging that then CEO David Glass had breached contracts and was liable for misrepresentations, deceptive trade practices, and injurious falsehood. The president of ADDvantage told his stockholders that their calculators had been "a huge success for Wal-Mart," and that the company was "shocked and disappointed" when Wal-Mart dropped them. The calculator company said Wal-Mart's decision was "wholly unexplained and unexpected." "Furthermore," they said, "it's a decision we find especially difficult to understand in view of our proven ability to increase Wal-Mart's advertised product movement . . . and the very enthusiastic support voiced in behalf of the program by Wal-Mart's management, their store managers, and their customers." Apparently all these endorsements by Wal-Mart officials didn't add up to enough in the Big Company's calculations. Wal-Mart's sudden decision left ADDvantage with a very big hole in its balance sheet.

"The retailer has a clear policy for suppliers," *Fast Company* concluded. "On basic products that don't change, the price Wal-Mart will pay, and will charge shoppers, must drop year after year. But what almost no one outside the world of Wal-Mart and its 21,000 suppliers knows is the high cost of those low prices."

Wal-Mart can wring out compromises from its suppliers. One of the first things to get cut is labor costs. The consequences of this reality has been felt by thousands of American workers — from the textile plants in North Carolina to the fabrication plants in Milwaukee.

On rare occasions, Wal-Mart vendors have challenged the giant retailer. In a number of high-profile disputes, Wal-Mart again has found itself in court, sued by some of the best-known brand names in America.

In the case *Nike v. Wal-Mart*, a U.S. District Court in Richmond, Virginia ordered Wal-Mart and its shoe supplier, Hawe Yue, to pay Nike a total of $6 million for infringement of Nike's design patent on its Air Mada outdoor shoe. Wal-Mart had been selling the cheaper, Korean knock-off shoes that looked very similar to the Nike brand. The court prohibited Wal-Mart from selling any more of the look-alike shoes.

Wal-Mart appealed the decision, and a Federal Circuit Court of Appeals cut the fine down to $1.4 million, arguing that under trademark law, Nike had to mark its patented products with a patent number, which Nike had failed to do. The court therefore limited the amount of damages that Nike could recover in the case to lost sales — not the profits that Wal-Mart made on sales of the knock-off shoes.

A number of other prominent manufacturers have had to go to court to prevent Wal-Mart from harming their company. Brand-name manufacturers like Tommy Hilfiger and Adidas have sued Wal-Mart. In April 2000, Adidas and Nike were in court to prevent Wal-Mart from selling T-shirts with phony logo brands. Both companies claimed Wal-Mart was selling several styles of counterfeit T-shirts at Sam's Clubs. In a similar lawsuit in 1998, Wal-Mart was charged with selling fake brand Hilfigers on its website. Wal-Mart paid Hilfiger $6.4 million to settle the lawsuit.

Three other major brands took Wal-Mart to court: Ralph Lauren, Nautica and Fubu. Wal-Mart settled the Polo and Nautica cases by paying out more than half a million dollars. Wal-Mart responded to these lawsuits by saying to *Reuters*, "We would never knowingly sell merchandise that was not

100% genuine." Claiming ignorance, Wal-Mart suggested that it was being duped by the vendors it does business with — yet the company claimed to scrutinize its suppliers to weed out the less-than-genuine. "If they can't prove it's authentic, we don't buy it," a Wal-Mart spokesman said.

But the lawsuits continue. Adidas issued a statement highly critical of Wal-Mart with the following warning to shoppers:

> Counterfeit sales by retailers like Wal-Mart are particularly troublesome to us, because the customer's guard is totally down. Anyone who walks into Sam's Club has no inkling that the goods he or she is buying may not be authentic.

In March 1999, Wal-Mart found itself embroiled in another product knock-off case. The popular British-born Teletubbies were making war on Bubbly Chubbies — a product sold on Wal-Mart shelves. It was a battle over the lucrative children's toy market.

The producers of Teletubbies, the bearish characters with televisions implanted in their stomachs, filed a lawsuit in Manhattan charging that Wal-Mart's Bubbly Chubbies were an unauthorized copy of the original Teletubbies.

But Wal-Mart, in its defense, said it required the makers of the Chubbies to give them a legal opinion which indicated that the Chubbies did not infringe on any trademark or copyright for the Tubbies. The Chubbies found a lawyer in Pittsburgh who was willing to say just that, and the look-alike, sound-alike imitations began selling at Wal-Mart stores.

But the Tubbies went after the Chubbies in court. The complaint charged:

> The Bubbly Chubbies characters are obvious, studied knock-offs of the famous Teletubbies characters. The name Bubbly Chubbies was deliberately chosen to rhyme with Teletubbies, and to communicate to children and their parents that the Bubbly Chubbies characters are chubby or tubby and have the same or similar attributes and evoke the same good will as the genuine Teletubbies.

Wal-Mart admitted, "Clearly, the item is similar to the Teletubbies products," which also could be found on Wal-Mart shelves. Shortly after the lawsuit was made public, Wal-Mart announced that a settlement had been reached. Wal-Mart agreed to pull the Chubbies off their shelves, and destroy whatever remaining inventory of Chubbies was left. England's Ragdoll Productions, and its American licensing agent, Itsy Bitsy Entertainment, got Wal-Mart to provide them with information about the manufacturing and distribution of the Chubbies. Wal-Mart said the Chubbies was just a "one-time purchase." To the media, Wal-Mart pointed out that it paid no monetary damages in the settlement. Itsy Bitsy Entertainment said money was never the object of the lawsuit — it was really about "protecting the integrity" of the Teletubbies' trademarks.

In a similar vein to "counterfeit" sales, Wal-Mart was caught trying to pass off used merchandise as new. In October 1999, in Visalia, California, Wal-Mart was caught trying to fool its customers. The company admitted that it had been passing off old goods as new to its unsuspecting shoppers. The admission, however, only came after the County's District Attorney filed a lawsuit alleging that Wal-Mart was charging customers full price for bicycles that had been returned by other customers.

According to the *Fresno Bee*, the District Attorney charged Wal-Mart employees with engaging in fraudulent business practices by selling returned bicycles at regular store prices, and not inspecting the bikes. The lawsuit noted that the uninspected bikes were then sold to other shoppers. The District Attorney said that Wal-Mart stores in Visalia, Tulare and Porterville were fraudulently selling returned bikes as new for over four years. The DA said that Wal-Mart declined to offer information about its bicycle sales during the investigation.

A Wal-Mart spokesman said its official policy is to inspect bikes when they are returned, and resell them at a reduced price. Wal-Mart's excuse for not following their own policy? Wal-Mart claimed it failed to communicate its own policy to its employees. "It was something that was a mistake and we feel was unique," said a Wal-Mart spokesman. "The bottom line is making sure that we take care of the customer." The DA sought $5,000 for each violation discovered, saying that customers "must be told the condition of any item they purchase." Revelations like this one put the phrase "taking care of the customer" in a new light.

# Count 4:
# Degrading the Environment

*"To be a serious statewide polluter at eleven stores gives Wal-Mart*
*a very dubious distinction as an environmental lawbreaker."*
— Connecticut Attorney General Richard Blumenthal, April 19, 2000

Wal-Mart's building of big-box superstores around the country comes with a tremendous environmental cost. Wal-Mart's new stores often have a deleterious effect on the local ecosystem.

A developer from Atlanta came to Valdosta, Georgia in 2000 and told local officials that their existing 123,000-square-foot Wal-Mart had "insufficient room" to remain competitive in the Valdosta trade area, so they wanted to build a new 219,000-square-foot superstore. The developer argued that Valdosta's population had grown by 9% between 1997 and 2002. A larger store would "allow Wal-Mart to attract more customers." Wal-Mart often says it needs bigger stores so that its customers can have "wider aisles."

But expanding the store would also allow Wal-Mart to destroy one acre of wetlands and a local streambed.

Area residents said that Wal-Mart was all wet. They challenged the developer's request to the U.S. Army Corps of Engineers under the Clean Water Act. As part of the application process, the developer had to explore alternative sites, including the re-use of an empty Kmart site. "Although this site satisfies many of the previously listed selection criteria," the developer admitted, "Kmart's policy of not selling property to their competitors excludes this site for consideration." In other words, the wetlands had to be filled in because Kmart wouldn't allow its dead store to be filled in — or so the developer claimed.

The developer went to a local stream mitigation bank to see how much it would cost to pay for the damage it would do to the Hightower Creek area wetland, but when the bank quoted $1.5 million, the developer balked and said the price tag was "not practicable and reasonable." Instead, they got the Valdosta City Council to approve the idea of stream mitigation projects at three other sites in the city.

Residents complained that there was absolutely no need for the Wetlands Wal-Mart in the first place, since the 50,000 community residents already had a Wal-Mart, a Wal-Mart supercenter, and a Sam's Club. "One of the other stores will be closed down and sit idle," warned the Valdosta/Lowndes County Alliance for Conserving Environmental Resources. "We will see the destruction of a natural stream and forested wetland occur almost simultaneous to the emergence of yet another idle concrete wasteland." The taxpayers said the city already had enough "ghost malls" and didn't need to create more.

The federal Clean Waters Act required the U.S. Army Corps of Engineers to review the benefits and detriments of this seemingly redundant project. The Corps was required to look at probable impacts of the project and its cumulative impact on public interest. There appeared to be very little interest in Valdosta in satisfying Wal-Mart's needs at the expense of a local stream and riparian wetland. The entire project would impact twenty acres, and have negative impacts on the economy and the aesthetics of Valdosta.

The developer was prepared to fill in wetlands — all to create a "useless wasteland of concrete." Rather than sit down and talk to Kmart about their dead site, the Valdosta City Councilors signed off on wasting undeveloped wetlands, even while "ghost malls" encircled the city.

The Valdosta story is painfully familiar to many communities across the country. Along with economic and social impacts, big box stores often trigger environmental damage that can range from pollution of streams or rivers due to storm water runoff, to destruction of wetlands, deterioration of air quality from traffic congestion, loss of open space and scenic vistas, and noise and light pollution.

An American Lung Association study conducted in 2000 found that air pollution caused largely by traffic congestion in Mecklenburg and Wake Counties in North Carolina had pushed these counties to 12th and 24th, respectively, among the top 25 counties in America with the worst air pollution. A Brookings Institute study released in the summer of 2000 revealed that the seven largest cities in North Carolina, facilitated by liberal annexation laws, had expanded their borders to capture 40% of the state's population growth in the 1990s. Sprawling developments increase pressure for more roads, more turning lanes, more traffic signals and ultimately, more federal money to fight air pollution.

In Connecticut, Attorney General Richard Blumenthal filed a lawsuit on April 19, 2000 against Wal-Mart over the issue of storm water pollution. The pollution at Wal-Mart comes from their frequent habit of storing fertilizers, pesticides and other pollutants outside their store, often in parking lot areas. Heavy rains then carry these pollutants as runoff from asphalt parking lots into nearby streams, ponds or rivers. Blumenthal announced that he had filed suit in Hartford Superior Court claiming that Wal-Mart had been polluting storm water in the state — not just at one or two stores, but at eleven separate Wal-Mart locations throughout Connecticut. "To be a serious statewide polluter at 11 stores gives Wal-Mart a very dubious distinction as an environmental lawbreaker," Blumenthal told *Reuters*. The Connecticut Environmental Protection Commissioner Arthur Rocque, Jr., told reporters that his office had made "repeated attempts" to get Wal-Mart to stop violating Connecticut's environmental laws. "Unfortunately," said Commissioner Rocque, "Wal-Mart has failed to take their environmental shortcomings seriously, and they continue to create conditions that adversely impact the state's natural resources."

Wal-Mart said it was surprised that the lawsuit was filed. "We've taken significant efforts to correct the problem," Wal-Mart noted, "which is why the suit is such a surprise...Because to assess civil penalties for something that happened last summer is to suggest that we've ignored the concerns of the state, which is absolutely not true. As soon as these incidents were brought to our attention last summer, we took significant efforts to rectify all these violations at each of our stores." Apparently whatever efforts Wal-Mart made at the 11 stores in question were not nearly enough to prevent state officials from hauling Wal-Mart into Superior Court.

Because Wal-Mart often uses its parking lots as a sales and storage area for garden supplies, including pesticides and fertilizers, communities have grown protective of their ground water and streams. In Connecticut, environmental officials determined that Wal-Mart was a "serious statewide polluter" that "failed to take their environmental shortcomings seriously."

In February 2004, the U.S. Justice Department and Wal-Mart agreed to settle charges that the retailer's Sam's Club in 11 states had violated the Clean Air Act by selling refrigerants with chlorofluorocarbons, or CFCs, that leak from appliances and damage the earth's ozone layer. Sam's Club paid a $400,000 settlement to the government, and agreed to stop selling the products. "We make every effort to comply with all laws and regulations in every state that we do business," a Wal-Mart spokesperson told *Bloomberg News*. "We've already addressed the alleged violations and made a business decision to stop selling the Freon products in question to our clubs over a year ago." But it took months of negotiations, and active intervention by the Justice Department to make Wal-Mart clean up its act. In the end, the company described the Freon settlement not as a victory for the environment – but a "business decision."

In June 2001, the U.S. Justice Department and the Environmental Protection Agency announced a settlement with Wal-Mart over allegations that the company had violated the Clean Water Act at eleven construction sites in Texas and six additional sites in New Mexico, Oklahoma and Massachusetts.

According to the EPA, Wal-Mart and ten of its contractors failed to comply with storm water regulations, and illegally discharged pollution from several construction sites. Wal-Mart responded by pointing out that the 17 sites mentioned by the government were just a fraction of the 300 or more new stores that Wal-Mart builds each year. But according to the Justice Department, the settlement with Wal-Mart was the first federal enforcement action against a company with multi-state violations of the storm water provisions of the Clean Water Act.

Under the settlement, Wal-Mart and its contractors agreed to pay a $1 million civil penalty and set up an environmental management plan to improve its procedures with environmental laws at its construction sites. The Justice Department estimated that this environmental management plan would cost Wal-Mart $4.5 million. Wal-Mart also agreed to require its construction contractors to assure that they have met storm water runoff guidelines before beginning construction. Wal-Mart told EPA officials that they would more carefully monitor construction sites for any storm water pollution.

But Wal-Mart developers frequently select environmentally

sensitive areas on which to build. In April 2000, Wal-Mart announced plans for a supercenter right on the edge of the nation's oldest archaeological preserve, the Casa Grande Ruins National Monument in southern Arizona. 650 years ago, the Hohokam Indians constructed "Great Houses" out of the concrete-like caliche mud. Wal-Mart proposed to move in as a neighbor, with a 107,000-square-foot store that might not last more than 10 years, much less five centuries. Local officials in Coolidge, Arizona seemed content to require the supercenter to be colored with earth tones. "We didn't want to see any 40-foot neon Indians with a tomahawk," the Superintendent of the Monument told the *Associated Press*. Instead, they got a big box retailer wrapped in a building constructed for only $30 per square foot, the epitome of the transitory modern age encroaching on ancient grounds. Wal-Mart wanted to locate across from the ruins to cash in on the 170,000 visitors the monument receives annually. A local merchant pointed out the obvious. "I hate to see sprawl. If they have to have it, move into town where we already have stuff, buy up these old lots, and build their development." But today, Wal-Mart supercenter # 2778 can be found on North Arizona Boulevard just a short distance from Ruins Drive.

Sometimes an environmental impact is obvious, immediate, and very personal. Richard Blowers owned a farm on Old Trail Road in Montgomery County, New York. In September 1999, contractors hired by Wal-Mart were using earth movers to prepare land near Blower's farm for the construction of a colossal 868,000-square-foot food distribution center in Johnstown, New York.

According to the *Metroland* newspaper, the earth movers did more than move dirt — they accidentally dug into the aquifer that supplied water to Blower's dairy farm. After the aquifer was drained, Blowers was forced to lay off his farm workers, and sell off most of his heifers, because his operation had no water for the animals.

Blowers fell behind with his suppliers, and he filed for bankruptcy. His lawyer said that Blowers and his company filed for Chapter 11 protection. "Basically [the farm] used to run on a milk check," the attorney said. "They had heifers that would raise young cows so they'd become milkers one day. The absence of sufficient water has caused his operations to abandon milk production."

The attorney said that Wal-Mart drilled a new well on their land and tried to pipe water over to Blower's. "They have attempted to replace some of the water," Blower's lawyer told *Metroland*, "but it doesn't work." He explained that the New York Department of Agriculture and Markets considers piped-in water unfit for a dairy farm. "It's been very tragic," the Albany attorney added. "It's a family who've been farming, I guess, four or five generations." He said Blowers has suffered "significant anguish as well as economic injury."

Blower's lawyers said they attempted to negotiate with Wal-Mart over the financial devastation from the loss of the farm. "So far, those attempts have been unsuccessful, and I am reviewing his options," said his attorney. Shortly afterwards, the dairy farmer filed a lawsuit against Wal-Mart, charging that its distribution center had destroyed his subterranean aquifer, which was the main source of two spring-fed reservoirs on his property. The suit asked the court for $15 million in damages against Wal-Mart.

Much of this environmental and economic damage was created at taxpayer's expense, by the Empire State Development Corporation. Empire State assembled an incentive package for Wal-Mart that included a $650,000 capital grant, a $250,000 employee training grant, and $1 million in road infrastructure improvements, sales tax abatements and water facilities improvements. *Metroland* reported that when wetlands permits from the U.S. Army Corps of Engineers and the Fish and Wildlife Service got hung up, Wal-Mart got an assist from U.S. Senator Charles Schumer and Congressman John McHugh to speed up the federal approvals. The Blowers farm was just the first casualty of the Wal-Mart distribution center. Retail grocers throughout New York state were next.

# Count 5:
# Unfair Competition

*"Business is a competitive endeavor...Nobody owes anybody else a living."*
— Sam Walton, Made in America

For more than ten years, I have collected letters from small merchants around the country, recounting their close encounters with giant big box retailers like Wal-Mart.

One couple from Eufaula, Alabama told me that after Wal-Mart arrived, most of the small businesses in their little community closed and the historic downtown deteriorated. They lamented that a "Wal-Mart mentality" had set in: "This being that the only criteria for making a purchase decision anymore seems to be who has the cheapest product. Not quality, not service... just price."

This couple moved to Eufaula, Alabama back in 1981 and took over the wife's family sporting goods store. "We worked hard," they wrote, "relocated to an historic building downtown and our business thrived. Our nearest competition was the malls in Dothan and Columbus, nearly an hour away. But they kept us on our toes and we concentrated on high-end, quality merchandise."

Their business continued to grow, adding a screen printing shop, then moving to a new building out near the other centers. A year later they got word that Wal-Mart was coming. The couple hung in for about a year after Wal-Mart opened, then gave up in the summer of 1991. Luckily, their screen printing business survived and eventually evolved into the promotional products and graphics business they own today.

"We have watched a steady stream of small local business failures," the couple told me. "Some had been here for years. Some opened, struggled, then closed. Three sporting goods chains have opened stores here since we closed ours. Only one remains." The husband and wife ended their letter by saying, "So far, we are fortunate that Wal-Mart has not ventured into graphic design and advertising."

In May 2000, I received a letter from Ruston, Louisiana. It was from a woman who had supported her three grandchildren by running a knitting and needlepoint store. "One day," the woman wrote, "in the early 70s, a man came in the store and was looking around." The woman offered to help the stranger, but he said he was just looking. After a few minutes of close inspection, he asked the woman if the owner was in. The woman told the customer that she was the owner. He then introduced himself as Sam Walton and told her that he was building the new Wal-Mart out on the interstate and that he was going to put her out of business. He then turned and left.

It's no secret that Wal-Mart has spelled the demise of many small "mom and pop" businesses. Just about everything Wal-Mart has turned its hand to has turned to gold. Over the years, as Wal-Mart has moved into various product markets, like groceries or gas stations or cars, the existing retailers have often stated their skepticism that Wal-Mart would be unable to prosper in their market area. Many gas station operators stayed on the sidelines when department stores were going under. They said Wal-Mart meant more traffic going by their gas stations. But when Wal-Mart paired up with the Murphy Oil Company to begin installing gas stations in Wal-Mart and Sam's Club parking lots, the gas retailers were suddenly thrown into the battle. A study produced by Energy Analysis International projects that by 2005, big box gas outlets like Wal-Mart and supermarket chains will have 7,000 gas stations in their parking lots, and control 16% of total gasoline sales. According to the study, when companies like Wal-Mart sell gas, "If they sell a lot of gasoline, they don't need to make much money on every gallon." Stand-alone gas stations that sell gas as their main livelihood can not use the product as a loss leader. But to Wal-Mart, gas sales are just a hook to lure customers into their parking lots more often. Wal-Mart can even afford to take a loss on gasoline in order to drive up sales inside the store.

Customer traffic to Wal-Mart has exploded over the years, and most business analysts see no impediment to the domination by a few big chains over 21st century retailing. Federal anti-trust laws being what they are (ancient and Byzantine), there is not likely to be any Microsoft-style break-up effort aimed at Wal-Mart. An executive from the Starbucks chain — which itself has been increasingly criticized for encroaching on every street corner in America — differentiated itself from Wal-Mart. "We're not in the business of undercutting the price of commonly-available merchandise and putting existing retailers out of business," Scott Bedbury, Senior VP for Marketing for Starbucks, said in a 1996 interview in *Fortune* magazine.

In a 2003 study, the consulting firm Retail Forward made the warning very clear: "Wal-Mart will continue to steam roll the competitive landscape by building a portfolio of formats that capture all consumer food and drug trips. The company's aggressive expansion will continue to wreak havoc and steal share away from conventional food, drug, and mass retailers at an alarming pace."

At public hearings before local Zoning Boards across the country, the argument heard most often in favor of Wal-Mart is that it will bring much-needed "competition" to the community. But what, in fact, if Wal-Mart represents the end of competition in small town America?

Wal-Mart likes to roll out local Chambers of Commerce or town officials who will swear that the superstores have been good for local businesses. But the volume of email I receive tells another side of the "WAL."

Rodney Turner is probably kicking himself that he didn't see what was coming sooner. Turner owned an IGA grocery store in the city of Republic, Missouri. This small town of roughly 8,400 people can only support so many grocery stores. For the past 15 years, Turner was able to keep his IGA open. But on Saturday, January 11, 2003, the Republic IGA closed its doors forever. The arrival of a 158,000-square-foot Wal-Mart supercenter was the end of the line for Turner's IGA. "It was a combination of a lot of things," Turner told the *Springfield News-Leader*, "but when you come down to it, the supercenter's what put us over the edge." Turner told reporters, "We probably should have closed the store the minute they opened the supercenter."

But Turner, who owns two other grocery stores in Missouri, remained open for as long as he was able. He said the decision to close was a hard one to make after 15 years, but after floundering for a few months, he couldn't compete with the Wal-Mart supercenter. It only took 4 months to drive the independent IGA under. Turner is leaving Republic with a bitter taste in his mouth, because he feels town officials gave Wal-Mart a sweetheart deal that further strained the unfair advantage against him.

As if Wal-Mart's size advantage was not enough, the city gave the retailer corporate welfare as well. The city of Republic worked out a deal with Wal-Mart in which the city paid $550,000 in infrastructure improvements to the Wal-Mart Route 60 location. "Really, if it wasn't for the city giving them that money, I'd look at it as what's fair is fair," Turner explained. "But then to give them additional incentive to come, that's what makes it sour grapes for me." City officials responded to Turner's charges by admitting they knew Wal-Mart would put out some smaller, local businesses. "The overall economic benefit to the city as a whole is what the Board of Aldermen has to look at," said the City Administrator.

But Turner feels that the city may have hurt its own cause by paving the way for a supercenter. "There's probably a lot of small businesses that aren't even looking at Republic because it's got a supercenter," he said. The city sticks by its claim that Wal-Mart has created a "landslide of new development." In this case, the landslide buried the 15-year-old dream of Rodney Turner.

Wal-Mart says it's a "retail magnet." The company claims that when it comes to town, it creates an "incentive for customers to stay home and spend dollars within the community — not only at Wal-Mart, but at other local businesses as well." Ironically, merchants like Rodney Turner are the ones who keep more of their profits locally, when compared to the large chains. The problem in most small towns is that officials often can't tell the difference between growth and development. As the Rocky Mountain Institute explains:

> Growth and development are not the same. Growth is an increase in quantity, while development is an increase in quality. This distinction is particularly important to the residents of many growing communities who are learning the hard way that growth is not the solution to their economic woes. While they enjoy the benefits of growth, they also

are vexed by the problems it causes: higher taxes, traffic congestion, crime, long commutes, air pollution, increasing intolerance, disrespect for traditional leadership, increasingly cutthroat competition in local business, higher rents, housing shortages, spiraling costs, and demands for higher wages to meet the higher cost of living.

There is no premium placed on the investment of local funds in small businesses, versus national chain stores. The same officials who want to attract new business don't seem to understand how to take care of the businesses they already have. But, as the Institute notes, a dollar spent locally can become a dollar re-spent:

When a dollar enters a community and is then spent outside the community, its benefit is felt only once. If that same dollar is re-spent within the community, its benefit is multiplied: it adds more value, pays more wages, finances more investments, and ultimately creates more jobs. Thanks to this 'multiplier effect,' each additional transaction in which the dollar is involved creates just as much wealth as a new dollar from the outside, but relies on local decisions made by people who care about the community.

A study in 2003 by the Institute for Local Self Reliance and the Friends of Midcoast Maine concluded that local stores produce bigger economic benefits for local economies than big box superstores. According to *The Economic Impact of Locally Owned Businesses vs. Chains: A Case Study in Midcoast Maine*: "Three times as much money stays in the local economy when you buy goods and services from locally-owned businesses compared to chain stores." The study monitored the revenue and expenditures of eight locally-owned businesses in the Maine towns of Rockland, Camden, and Belfast. They represented a range of goods and services, and employed 62 people and had sales of $5.7 million in 2002.

The survey found that the businesses spent 44.6% of their revenue within the surrounding two counties. Another 8.7% was spent elsewhere in the state of Maine. The businesses spent their money locally on wages and benefits paid to local employees; goods and services purchased

47

from other local businesses; profits to local owners; and taxes paid to local and state government. Each of the surveyed businesses banked with locally owned banks, bought inventory from local manufacturers, advertised in local newspapers, and hired local accountants, printers, internet service providers and repair people. The other 46.7% of their revenue left the state, for inventory purchased out-of-state, mortgage interest, rent, credit card fees, supplies, insurance, and equipment leasing.

The study also looked at a major big box retailer with stores in Maine, using national data, company statements, and information from one of the chain's stores in Maine. "The analysis found that the chain returned only 14.1% of its revenue to the local economy, mostly in the form of payroll. The rest leaves the state, flowing to out-of-state suppliers or back to corporate headquarters."

The analysis recommended that expanding local businesses would be a better economic development strategy for the region than chasing after chain stores. Assuming retail sales in the three cities would expand by $74 million over the next four years, if all of this spending growth were captured by new and expanding locally-owned businesses, it would add $23 million more to the local economy each year than if all of the new spending were captured by chains.

The survey also concluded that the local businesses contributed more to charity than national chains. The eight businesses made $24,000 in cash donations, which amounts to 0.4% of their revenue. That's four times as much, relative to overall sales, as Wal-Mart gave to charity in 2002, and twice as much as Target gave, the study said.

There is a form of mathematics not taught in American public schools. I call it "Wal-Math." Economist Tom Muller has illustrated how "Wal-Math" operates in the real world. A retail sales impact report produced by Muller and Beth Humstone in 1993 regarding a proposed Wal-Mart in St. Albans, Vermont concluded that for every one job Wal-Mart created, 1.5 retail jobs elsewhere would be lost:

> In the first year of operation there will be no net losses of retail employment in the primary market area. However, over time the number of retail jobs in the county will decline by 200 jobs. This is

due to the fact that the existing retail businesses in Franklin County are more labor-intensive than Wal-Mart. For every $10,000,000 in sales in typical Franklin County retail businesses, 106 people are employed. For every $10,000,000 in sales at a typical Wal-Mart, 70 people are employed. Due to projected sales losses to existing businesses in Franklin County, there will be up to 500 retail jobs lost over the next ten years. These jobs will be offset partially by the gain of nearly 300 jobs over the same time period.

A similar economic impact study in 1998 in Sault Ste. Marie, Ontario concluded that a 106,000-square-foot Wal-Mart would produce "virtually no gain in employment." The study indicated that the overall project, which included a total of 300,000 square feet of retail space would create — and destroy — jobs:

| | |
|---|---|
| Wal-Mart employment | 129 |
| Other retail employment | + 387 |
| Total Project | 516 |
| Job Decline Elsewhere | - 485 |
| Net Gain from project | 31 |

Ninety-four percent of the job gains would be lost elsewhere in the community. The study said, "Existing retail establishments may lose almost 500 jobs in response to lower sales." The report added that the final impact could be even worse than stated, since the employment losses at other stores were understated. "For the same dollar for dollar loss in sales elsewhere in Sault Ste. Marie, the resulting employment loss could be higher," because discount stores employ fewer employees per sales levels.

If Wal-Mart represents a form of economic displacement, not economic development, it's not something they like to talk about. Except to their own people. In the October 1996 issue of *Wal-Mart Today*, an internal associate newsletter that Wal-Mart bills as "your window into our Wal-Mart world," there is a column called "Wal-Mart Culture." In it is a quote that should be written on the side of every Wal-Mart superstore in the nation:

"At Wal-Mart, we make dust. Our competitors eat dust."
— Tom Coughlin, Executive Vice President, Operations, Wal-Mart
Stores Division

Coughlin is currently President and CEO of Wal-Mart Stores Division.
Since 1962, the Wal-Mart dust machine has been grinding through retailers
in every state in the country. Wal-Mart has cannibalized the retail food
chain from the Mom and Pops on the bottom, to the mid-level regional
chains, to the very top national chains.

In the grocery store field, Wal-Mart superstores have left many
competitors hungry for sales. According to the consulting firm Retail
Forward, in the decade between 1992 and 2002, the grocery industry
lost 13,000 stores, or 17% of the industry. These were not all Mom and
Pop stores. Even the big chains were thinned out. The Florida-based
Winn-Dixie supermarkets announced in April 2000 the elimination of
11,000 jobs as a cost-cutting move, roughly 8% of its 132,000-person
workforce. At the time, Winn-Dixie was the sixth largest grocery chain
in the U.S. with stores in 14 states and the Bahamas. Most of its holdings
were in the Dixieland South. The workers who lost their jobs were in
114 of the company's 1,189 locations. The company announced it was
"retiring" 10 vice presidents, but as the *Associated Press* noted: "Store
workers will bear the brunt of the layoffs."

In most stories about these layoffs, Wal-Mart was cited as a major
reason for the Winn-Dixie losses. "The U.S. supermarket industry has
been consolidating in a bid by larger grocers to compete more effectively
with each other as well as Wal-Mart Stores, which has moved aggressively
into the food business at its massive store network in the U.S.," said the
*Associated Press*. *Reuters* added that Wal-Mart "became the No. 5 U.S.
seller of groceries during the 1990s by expanding mainly in Winn-Dixie's
backyard in the southern U.S."

An average Winn-Dixie store has 85 workers, the company said,
but would not disclose a list of doomed stores. Earlier in the year Winn-
Dixie sold 74 stores to Kroger, at that time the largest U.S. grocer.
The shrinking of Winn-Dixie was supposed to save the company $400
million a year. 11,000 families were "trimmed" from the company,
like so much fat from a steak. And Wal-Mart held the knife. "Today's

grocery business is probably the most competitive in our 75-year history," the chairman of Winn-Dixie told the media. The company said the workers losing their jobs would be notified as "expeditiously as possible and [stores would be] closed as expeditiously as possible."

In the Winn-Dixie story, the consumer was the ultimate loser. Wal-Mart often comes to small towns promising, "Wal-Mart brings in traffic and customers to the area," and local officials believe the mantra. They believe that building more grocery stores will make people hungrier. But what happened to the workers at Winn-Dixie is the reality. Wal-Mart had a hunger for Winn-Dixie's market share, and the result was 11,000 families out of work.

The list of fatalities gets longer. In March 2002, Kmart imploded. The shutting down of 271 Kmart discount stores and 12 Kmart supercenters largely became Wal-Mart's gain. In fact, Wal-Mart indicated some interest in grabbing up the dead Kmart locations (to build new stores, of course, and to keep the competition from leasing them). But if you look at the Kmart closings of these "underperforming" stores from the perspective of the economy — not the company — then you realize that the loss of 284 stores across 40 states and Puerto Rico, and the loss of 22,000 jobs, is a major offset in the economic "gain" that Wal-Mart claims for the economy. In fact, the shutting down of 284 stores nullifies the "growth" of nearly 3 years of Wal-Mart stores, and the destruction of 22,000 jobs means that the next 50 supercenters that Wal-Mart builds bring no new added value to the economy.

Kmart described its losses as "enhancements" to its cash flow by nearly $550 million. Analysts often describe bankruptcy as an opportunity for the corporation to mend its unprofitable ways, so that it can "re-emerge" from Chapter 11 better from the experience. But it was an experience that killed the cash flow of 22,000 families, and caused secondary impacts on businesses located in malls and nearby locations, as well as other businesses that depended on providing professional services to Kmart— everyone from local newspapers to cleaning services. Kmart said in a press release that it deeply regretted the impact of these store closings on its workers, its customers and "the communities where these stores are located." The states that were double-digit losers included Texas, where 33 Kmarts closed; Illinois (21); the corporation's home state of Michigan

(18); California and Florida (16 each); Georgia (14); and Ohio (10). The day after Kmart filed for Chapter 11 protection, Wal-Mart opened 17 new stores in 12 states. A week later they opened another 5 Wal-Marts. The *Charlotte Observer* wrote, "Now, as Kmart prepares to close some stores, [Wal-Mart] has the opportunity to raise prices and increase profits." The *Observer* quoted Joe Engebretson, who helps manage $300 million for Engebretson Capital Management, that Wal-Mart would now be able to move toward more of a monopoly.

In May 2003, Kmart re-emerged out of Chapter 11 bankruptcy — but not before closing hundreds of stores and harming thousands of workers. Maybe the "leaner" Kmart will survive, but an enormous amount of damage has already been done.

The lesson in sprawl-math seems inevitable: When you over-supply an area with retail glut, you don't create jobs, you destroy them. When Caldor Corporation imploded, industry analysts said it was expected. Caldor was losing money to Wal-Mart, had fallen into Chapter 11 territory since 1995, and never recovered. As one news story said: "Wal-Mart and other rivals had choked off Caldor's ability to open stores outside its traditional Northeast territory."

All over the country, from below the Mason/Dixon line to the Plains states and California, many of the "Belle Epoch" names in retailing were gone, victims of an elaborate game of retail musical chairs. When the music stopped, tens of thousands of workers were left stranded on the dance floor without a partner.

The phenomenon of super-saturation of giant chain stores has been called "the Wal-Mart effect." Although Wal-Mart likes to assert that it is a "retail magnet" attracting more sales to a community, enhancing the business environment, adding jobs, revenues, and lifting all boats, the reality is exactly the opposite.

A company called Global Credit Services released a 7-page report in May 2000 that concluded, "The disproportionate size of Wal-Mart relative to its rivals in the distribution and retailing of finished goods represents a fundamental imbalance in the macroeconomy for the consumption of finished goods on a global basis." GCS also said, "The risk for these systemic imbalances is that a large number of retailing and distribution firms will be forced to either merge or file bankruptcy and in some instances these firms will terminate their operations." GCS describes Wal-Mart as "a distribution firm at the center, and a mass merchandiser at the end of its own supply chain...Wal-Mart, in this sense, is the supreme disintermediator of the supply chain."

The GCS report continued: "It is well known that local merchants are often unable to survive against this imbalance in the local commerce of finished goods. Local shoppers disgorge so much of their discretionary earnings that they are not able to leverage enough additional personal consumption expenditures to support local merchants." GCS noted that this "imbalance" has created "sudden consolidations" in the supermarket field, and a "decline in the number of viable firms in the retail sale of discount apparel." All of this is due to what GCS simply labeled "the Wal-Mart effect."

"Any firm involved in the sale of most categories of nondurable finished goods has to deal with the Wal-Mart effect," the report added.

> The Wal-Mart effect says that so many dollars of finished goods are flowing through Wal-Mart to consumers that many other retailing firms will not be able to generate the level of revenue growth necessary to help fund their debts. There is not enough residual dollars left in the consumer economy to support a retailing firm the size of Wal-Mart and concurrently support a large number of other retailing firms...Wal-Mart stores are so large in scale that the low savings rate of consumers combined with rising levels of consumer credit must eventually lead to an increase in unfavorable conditions for a large number of retailing firms. Before more Wal-Mart shoppers give up on going to Wal-Mart for basics at daily low prices in a one-stop shopping experience, they will probably cease going to enough other stores to cause some problem at other firms.

In other words, Wal-Mart takes such a large market share that there is very little pie left for other merchants. Wal-Mart sucks up enough dollars that only "residual dollars" are left for other merchants.

In the summer of 1999, when Wal-Mart acquired its first foothold in England by purchasing the ASDA food store chain, one stock analyst told *Reuters*, "For the industry as a whole, it's not a bullish situation because Wal-Mart is very price-driven and they tend to take a bite out of the margin wherever they go. There will be a smaller cake of profit to share around and Wal-Mart will have quite a big slice of it."

Most of Wal-Mart's big slice has come from somebody else's pie. The evidence of competition withering is found in every small town and along every highway in America. In August 2003, a study by the consulting firm Customer Growth Partners concluded that mall-based stores had lost half their share of the retail market since 1995. Department stores, specialty retailers, and other chains that occupy shopping malls accounted for 38% of retail sales in 1995, but by 2002, their market share had plummeted to 19%.

The study found that the 40 largest American retailers took in $766 billion in sales in 2002 — of which 80% fell into the cash registers of "stand alone" retailers, like the big box Wal-Mart stores. "We may not be hearing the death knell of the mall, but we are seeing the long, slow demise of the mall as traditionally conceived," the Customer Growth Partners report said. "Consumers today neither have the time nor the patience to battle the parking space, teen-age crowd and in-store navigation hassles so typical of traditional malls and department stores," the report noted. The study compared department stores to "dinosaurs, as out of step with today's consumers as rotary-dial telephones and vinyl record albums."

Grocer Ron Dennis knows first-hand quite a bit about the Wal-Mart effect. He is not an economist, but as the President and Chief Operating Officer of Farm Fresh grocery stores in Virginia, he knows something about the price of bananas.

When Dennis visited his Farm Fresh store in Suffolk, Virginia in June of 2003, he noticed that the Wal-Mart supercenter across the street was selling bananas at 33 cents a pound. On the same day, he drove twenty miles away to Franklin, Virginia — where there is no Farm Fresh store competing with Wal-Mart. In Franklin, Wal-Mart was selling the same pound of bananas for 49 cents a pound. In Franklin, where competition was weak, the price of bananas at Wal-Mart was 48% higher than the Wal-Mart store in Suffolk.

Farm Fresh stores have pedestal signs located throughout the aisles that compare the company's prices to those at Wal-Mart, Food Lion, Harris Teeter and Kroger. But to Ron Dennis, the issue goes beyond prices. He likes to remind consumers that the quality of products he carries are often superior to Wal-Mart. Meat is one of his prime examples: "Don't you really want the best quality meats, and the best value for your hard-earned dollars?" one sign in his store reads. "Farm Fresh sells only USDA Choice and Certified Angus Beef." The sign shows a picture of meat purchased at Wal-Mart that says: "Injected with 12% solution?" and in smaller print: "Other stores sell pre-packaged 'fresh' meat that is cut in meat factories and shipped hundreds of miles — as far away as South Dakota! Other stores inject their beef with over 12% salt and water. Do you know that you are paying for salt and water?"

Wal-Mart changed to case-ready meats in 2001, enhancing their meat with added liquid. "We are always looking at ways to provide our customers with quality products at low prices," a Wal-Mart spokesman told the *Atlanta Journal Constitution* in December 2003. "We thought it was a good fit for us and our customers."

"It's a terrible trend," cookbook author Bruce Aidells told the *Journal Constitution*. "Whenever a meat company can sell you water at the price of meat, they're winning." A 2002 study by the Food Marketing Institute found that 60% of shoppers have no idea that their meat products are injected with salt water. Wal-Mart shifted to pre-cut meat 11 days after a group of meat-cutters in a Texas Wal-Mart voted to unionize. Wal-Mart managed to trim off the union, and consumers paid meat prices for water — another example of a Wal-Mart win-win solution.

Wal-Mart's advertising pitch suggested to shoppers that its prices were the lowest, all the time. But when competitors and the National Advertising Review Board challenged Wal-Mart to justify its slogan, "Always the low price, always," Wal-Mart responded by dropping the slogan. The NARB, which is made up of 70 advertising professionals, told Wal-Mart that they should eliminate any references to "the low price." Instead, the Board recommended that any modified slogan refrain from stating or implying that Wal-Mart prices are "always the lowest."

One internal document from a wholesale food distributor competing with Wal-Mart describes Wal-Mart's pricing policy as follows: "Wal-Mart will be as low or lower than the competition on all similar items they carry. It has never been Wal-Mart's intention to beat the competition on every item." In their grocery department, "Wal-Mart will never be undersold by any competitor. If a competitor has a lower price on any item, Wal-Mart will meet that price. Store managers have the authority to lower prices to meet or beat any competitor. Store managers must regularly check their competitors and react to any changes."

Wal-Mart maintains a list of 850 NBB — "never be beat" — products. It is the management's responsibility to guarantee customers always perceive them to be the low price leader. Wal-Mart will not be undersold on their NBB items. One competitor explained to me how Wal-Mart's pricing policy works:

> If Kraft Miracle Whip is at $1.97 at Wal-Mart, and the competition price is $1.78, Wal-Mart will meet that $1.78 price and spread lower prices to like items within the category on items such as Hellmann's and Kraft Mayonnaise, etc. In the event a competitor raises its price, the Wal-Mart store manager may also raise its price to meet competition up to the Wal-Mart established price. Under no circumstances can a Wal-Mart manager initiate a price increase or raise the price above a Wal-Mart established price. Wal-Mart will meet the competition and spread two additional key items within the category to maintain a 5% competitive advantage. If Tide detergent is at $3.47 at Wal-Mart, and the competition's price is $3.28, Wal-Mart will meet the $3.28 price and spread lower prices to like items within the category such as Cheer, Fab, Era, Rinso, etc. If an item is below base price and Wal-Mart meets this low price, they will spread two additional key items within the category to maintain a 5% competitive advantage.

Wal-Mart also has pricing loss leaders — popular items like baby formula, motor oil, diapers, and cigarettes — that the company is willing to drop down to ridiculously low prices in order to increase store traffic. Under no circumstances, the wholesaler said, are Wal-Mart stores, Sam's Clubs or supercenters to engage in competitive pricing against each other. However, with stores located only several miles from on another, it is inevitable that such stores will cannibalize each other's sales. The company understands, and encourages, such cannibalization.

The key principle behind Wal-Mart's "EDLP" (everyday low pricing) is that prices are based on the level of competition in that given community at that given time. In a diverse marketplace, Wal-Mart's prices are kept down only because of the company of other players. This explains the preoccupation with constantly monitoring the other retailers' prices. But as those other players die off, the pressure on pricing eases up, allowing prices to float higher.

Wal-Mart is absolutely obsessed with other stores' prices. Wal-Mart's pricing policy requires the company to constantly send its people out into the community to check prices at other stores. Associates are trained to perform certain tasks that other workers might find morally questionable. Wal-Mart management has to check competitive prices weekly, and a market basket of goods must be surveyed every month. These surveillance missions are randomly selected, highly recognizable price-sensitive items, including Wal-Mart's "Never Be Beat" list. Managers maintain a list of their competitors' current pricing and respond to price fluctuations at other stores. In an intensely competitive environment, Wal-Mart requires its people to make daily price checks. It is the assistant manager's responsibility to ensure that price checking the competition and reviewing the competition list is reported weekly to the department and zone managers.

When Wal-Mart employees are sent out to do price checks on the competition, they are equipped like secret agents in a James Bond movie. They may carry pocket-sized, voice-activated tape recorders with tie clip microphones. They have their "Never Be Beat" list with Universal Pricing Code (UPC) numbers. They carry hand-held scanning devices, which scan the UPC and enter the competitor's pricing. The scanner is about the size of a hand-held cassette recorder.

When I was in the midwest meeting with grocery store owners, they told me that as a courtesy to their competitors, they would often pre-arrange a time for the competition to openly go through their stores to scan prices. In return, they expected the same courtesy back from their neighboring stores. This shared scanning of prices was considered a professional courtesy of doing business. "Tell us you're coming and we'll set it up for you," was the response of one grocery store owner. "We'd tell them when to come, and ask them to complete their work in one or two hours."

But at Wal-Mart, the company secretly scans prices from its

competitors, yet escorts out any competitors who try to do the same
to them. Wal-Mart's policy is that it has extended a "license" to the
general public to enter into their stores for the purpose of purchasing or
examining the merchandise as a normal part of making purchases. But
any person in the employ of a competitor who enters a Wal-Mart for a
purpose other than buying items, does not have such a license, and, in
fact, is forbidden in any manner to record data concerning their prices or
the operation of the store. Any employee of a competitor who is caught
recording such data inside the store will immediately be asked to stop
recording, and escorted off the premises. This Wal-Mart policy on price
checking is supposed to be posted at the Courtesy Desk of every store.

This can create some occasional awkwardness for Wal-Mart. As
another company pointed out:

> They must realize that occasionally a customer will write
> down prices while shopping. Before they initiate a confrontation, they
> must be sure that the person taking down prices is a representative
> of a competitor. If they have any doubt about whether this person is
> recording prices for a competitor, they are to follow the "confrontation
> guidelines:" They simply approach the person with a friendly
> attitude and ask if they can help. They try not to antagonize the
> customer by confronting them in a manner that may offend them.
> Wal-Mart maintains that "all customers have the right and are invited
> to write down prices."

Edna Vinton was a Wal-Mart employee in Hearne, Texas. She
knows firsthand about price checking. "I was proud to work there for
awhile, and then later I was kind of ashamed that I did, because they
were closing down the stores that were here, and this is my home town.
I just hated what Wal-Mart did to Hearne." Vinton had to do "comp
pricing" at the competitors in town:

> The department managers had to go out every week and do
> what Wal-Mart calls 'comp pricing.' If you were in charge of ladies
> wear, you went to see if they had any clothing in town that was
> similar or the same brand as yours and what it was selling for. If it

was cheaper than yours, you came back and made it cheaper than theirs. And this was true in every department: health and beauty aids, food department, clothing department — every department in the store. We had to meet comp pricing. First, we'd go down to comp prices. If Kay Woolens had something at the same price we had it, we would lower it down to that price. You'd go back three days later, maybe, and if they had dropped it a little bit further, then you'd drop it drastically. Like if they dropped it to $9.96, then you'd drop it maybe to $6.96.

These smaller stores can not compete with that. Wal-Mart can, because they write it off. We lost the little stores, and then Wal-Mart is sitting out there with the prices jacked back up to where they were to begin with. So, you have no choice: if there's no little store to buy it from, and you need that item, then you pay Wal-Mart prices.

When Wal-Mart destroyed the competition, then they raised the prices back up to the original price. We not only lost businesses, we lost good citizens. And that's Wal-Mart's fault. I would warn any community not to allow Wal-Mart to come into your town. They destroy what business you do have.

When it comes to competition, it seems that Wal-Mart can dish it out — but not take it. In Davenport, Iowa, Wal-Mart found itself in a "tables turned" situation. The Wal-Mart store manager in Davenport told city officials in March 2001 that a SuperTarget was going to open across the street from his 110,000-square-foot Wal-Mart discount store, and therefore his company needed to leave its current site and open up a 220,000-square-foot superstore to be competitive. "I can't compete with that," Wal-Mart manager Tony Ciabattoni told the *Quad City Times*. "All we're asking for is a level playing field." Small merchants have been asking for three decades for a level playing field, but Wal-Mart has all but destroyed it.

Sam Walton may have been the most compulsive price checker at Wal-Mart. It was an obsession that he apparently passed down to his heirs in the Wal-Mart corporate family.

On May 17, 2000, inside the Crest Foods supermarket in Edmund, Oklahoma, the mood was somber and tense. Crest is a low-budget grocery operation. It brings low prices to its customers by not advertising, and by purchasing directly from manufacturers as much as possible. The manager and his staff were very conscious of what was happening just two miles away at the grand opening of a Wal-Mart supercenter in Edmund.

Sometime that afternoon, the Crest manager noticed a group of men enter his store. He observed that some of these people were holding hand-held electronic scanners. They were scanning prices at Crest Foods, to record them back home at the Wal-Mart supercenter. All of this activity was being captured on the Crest Food stores security cameras.

A store employee came up to the group and politely asked them to leave, which they did. But Wal-Mart employees came back repeatedly, sometimes to scan prices, other times to directly try to recruit Crest employees to come work at the new Wal-Mart supercenter.

Six days later, five Wal-Mart representatives entered Crest Foods again. The security cameras captured every movement. The assistant manager believed they were scanning Crest prices again. He asked them to leave the store. Then a senior manager from Crest approached the group, and told them that they were free to stay and look around the store, but that the assistant manager had simply not wanted them to scan Crest prices.

At that point, the group left the store.

Neither the Crest assistant manager, nor the senior manager, had any inkling that among the group of five from Wal-Mart, was David Glass, who by this date was Wal-Mart's immediate past president and CEO.

Crest employees later told their lawyers that Mr. Glass was "personally offended that he was 'kicked out' of Crest, even though he was subsequently invited to stay." Crest managers claim that Glass went back and ordered his Edmund supercenter "to obtain revenge by dropping its prices even below cost if necessary to drive Crest out of business."

These claims are contained in a complaint filed in the U.S. District Court for the Western District of Oklahoma in September 2000, alleging that Wal-Mart violated the federal Sherman Act, the Oklahoma Unfair Sales Act, and the Oklahoma Antitrust Reform Act.

Crest charged that from the day Glass visited their store, the Wal-Mart superstore in Edmund lowered its prices on "sensitive items" — like bread, milk and orange juice — "by consistently pricing them significantly below even the prices of the other Wal-Mart supercenters in the Oklahoma

City area, violating Wal-Mart's own pricing policy." Crest said that Wal-Mart held its prices for these items below their cost for significant periods of time, and that these "below-cost" prices were illegal, and prevented Crest from competing fairly with the Edmund supercenter.

Crest said that Wal-Mart, at Glass' direction, was selling below cost "with the intent and purpose of unfairly diverting trade from a competitor or otherwise injuring a competitor, impairing and preventing fair competition, or injuring public welfare."

"In particular," Crest concludes, "Wal-Mart had the specific intent to drive Crest out of business according to the mandate of Mr. Glass." Crest also accused Wal-Mart of violating the Antitrust Reform Act because its action "has a pernicious effect on competition and lacks any redeeming virtue."

Crest claimed that what Wal-Mart was trying to do was "achieve a monopoly in the market...[and] given Wal-Mart's market power in this market, there is a dangerous probability of Wal-Mart achieving a monopoly."

David Glass must have learned his price snooping at the foot of Sam Walton. Walton carried around with him a "little tape recorder" to take down prices. Walton wrote about being nabbed inside a Price Club store in California where they confiscated his recorder. "We have the same policy," Walton confessed, "and I knew I was caught." Walton jotted down a note to the store manager, pleading to get his tape back. About four days later, Walton's tape recorder was sent back to him, with nothing erased. "He probably treated me better than I deserved," Walton admitted.

Wal-Mart's obsession with price mirrors the consumers' obsession with price. The number one reason people shop at Wal-Mart is price. But hidden behind Wal-Mart's "falling prices" is a paradox that shoppers never see. Officials at the United Food and Commercial Workers union produced a study in December 1999 showing that food prices continued to rise as Wal-Mart shares in local grocery markets increased. In Columbia, South Carolina, for example, Wal-Mart's share of the food market rose from 0% to 7.6% between 1992 and 1999, yet food prices rose 1,200% higher than the cost of living. In Little Rock, Arkansas, Wal-Mart's home state, Wal-Mart's food share of the market rose from 0% to 11.3% from 1992 to 1999, yet food prices rose 337% higher than the cost of living. "Wal-Mart tells us 'Always,'" said the President of the

Nevada Council of Senior Citizens. "But when you look at what Wal-Mart does, you have to ask: Always a scam?"

In 1993, three drug stores in Conway, Arkansas sued Wal-Mart over alleged predatory pricing of health and beauty care products and over-the-counter drugs. The drug stores charged that Wal-Mart was selling these items below cost at their Conway supercenter. The drug stores claimed that Wal-Mart had violated a 1937 Arkansas Unfair Practices Act.

During the trial, in court depositions, Wal-Mart employees admitted that their company set prices based on how much competition it faced: more competition meant lower prices. During the court proceedings, according to the *Economist* newspaper, the judge found evidence that Wal-Mart would "lift its prices as and when competitors disappeared. Nearer to Little Rock, where there are plenty of pharmacies, its drug prices are lower; in more remote towns than Conway, they are higher." One example cited in the Arkansas case was evidence that Wal-Mart charged $11 for baby formula in Little Rock, while in the rural community of Flippin, Arkansas, the same product was priced at $22. A Chancery Court agreed with the druggists, but a higher court later ruled in Wal-Mart's favor.

In 1986, Wal-Mart lost a similar suit in Oklahoma. The company had violated a state law requiring retailers to sell goods at least 6.75% above cost, except during a sale or to match competitor's prices. There was an out-of-court settlement in the case, and Wal-Mart raised its prices. The retailer also spent $80,000 to lobby the Oklahoma state legislature to overturn the law. It was unsuccessful.

Four years later, in September 2000, German officials ordered Wal-Mart and two other indigenous retailers to stop holding down prices below wholesale. This no doubt sounded counter-intuitive to most Americans, since everyday low prices are the cornerstone of Wal-Mart's raison d'être. But for consumers, there can be "too much of a good thing" — low pricing that actually harms competition. That's the heart of the Wal-Mart pricing paradox. The major American press took this story about the German Cartel Office slapping Wal-Mart's hands, and ran headlines like "Wal-Mart told to raise prices." The Germans determined that Wal-Mart had been selling milk, butter, flour, cooking oil and other products below cost on a regular, sustained basis. The last phrase is crucial: on a regular basis. The Cartel Office said: "The material benefit [of below-cost pricing] to consumers is marginal and temporary, but the restriction of competition by placing unfair obstacles before medium-sized retailers is clear and lasting."

Here's the Wal-Mart paradox: everyday low prices are based on healthy competition in the marketplace. Competition among relative equals is more likely to resemble competition than among unequals. Yet as Wal-Mart enters a market, with its "Never Be Beat" list of 1,000 products, Wal-Mart becomes the engine that destroys competition, rather than fostering it. This is essentially what the Germans were upset about: Wal-Mart's below cost pricing gives the consumer a short high, followed by "clear and lasting" harm. You can measure that harm, for example, in the loss of 13,000 grocery stores since 1992. Or, you can measure that harm by manufacturing jobs lost in the economy, and the lowering of retail wages.

American reporters spun this German Cartel story to make it sound like German law was "heavily tilted toward protecting small shopkeepers," and made Wal-Mart sound like the victim. The reality is just the reverse. In this country, you need an army of anti-trust lawyers, a small fortune, and years of patience to attempt to bring a predatory pricing suit against anyone. The Germans have an easier time labeling predatory pricing for what it is: anti-consumer.

The "price paradox" of Wal-Mart is that consumers need the regional and smaller merchants to create competition in local markets. If Wal-Mart succeeds in making "our competitors eat dust," then it is the consumer who ultimately eats dust, as those everyday low prices become everyday mediocre prices. The smaller merchants are needed as counterbalances against Wal-Mart's dominating presence in small markets. So the German action, taken to help consumers, must have appeared to many Americans to be an action that hurt consumers. The paradox of forcing a company to raise prices as a means of ultimately keeping prices competitive is not likely to sink in to the 138 million Americans who disgorge their incomes at the Wal-Mart shrine each week. To the American press, Germany was just a "highly-regulated" economy with unhappy shoppers. All Wal-Mart was willing to say for the record was they would "orient our pricing in line with these recommendations," but cynically added that Wal-Mart "remains committed to lowering the cost of living in Germany." Apparently German officials saw it just the opposite: Wal-Mart represented clear and lasting damage to retailing competition. You won't find the Federal Trade Commission being as blunt.

Wal-Mart's rough handling in Germany on the pricing issue didn't seem to have much spillover effect in small town America. Wal-Mart ran smack into the same charge in five Wisconsin communities. According to the *Milwaukee Journal Sentinel*, Wal-Mart was charged on September 25, 2000 with cutting prices at a number of its stores to illegally take business from competitors. As in Germany, Wal-Mart was low-balling basic staples like milk, butter, detergent and cigarettes. Investigators from the Wisconsin Division of Trade and Consumer Protection detected below-cost pricing at Wal-Marts in West Bend, Racine, Beloit, Tomah and Oshkosh. According to Wisconsin state law, retailers cannot sell items at below cost to unfairly take business away from competitors. Wal-Mart's response was to claim the company was only reacting to price cuts by other retailers.

Responding to a price cut is legal — but initiating predatory pricing is not. The fundamental problem with Wal-Mart's claim was that they had no proof or records of initiation of price drops at other stores. "We did not take the initiative of lowering prices below cost," Wal-Mart claimed. "We acknowledge our record-keeping needs to improve." Wal-Mart told the *Journal Sentinel* that it had implemented a change in its computer program to document below-cost prices. But Wisconsin officials tell a different story: they went after Wal-Mart only after the company kept up the predatory practice — having been warned to stop since 1993. Under Wisconsin law, Wal-Mart faced a fine of $500 per violation for each of the 350 violations listed by state regulators. The state sought a court injunction to stop Wal-Mart's below-cost selling. If Wal-Mart continued to predatory price, the cost of each violation would rise to $5,000.

The company and Wisconsin reached a settlement in which Wal-Mart agreed to comply with the state's fair pricing law. Wal-Mart never admitted any wrongdoing in the case, and never paid a penalty. But if, in the future, the company were found violating its agreement, they would face double and triple the regular fines. Wal-Mart also agreed to make a $15,000 donation to a high school consumer education contest — an amount that covered the cost of Wisconsin's investigation. The company also agreed to create an internal price-tracking system that state auditors could use to ensure that Wal-Mart was complying with the agreement. A Wal-Mart spokesman told reporters: "We have made some changes to our record keeping in Wisconsin, and reiterated our desire to price our products as low as possible within the law."

All across America, millions of shoppers will steer their shopping carts through the Wal-Mart aisles this week, looking for a cheap pair of running shoes, or an electric can opener. Behind each price tag is a string of misfortunes that have befallen people, companies and economies. Wal-Mart success is like a billboard pasted over the failures of others.

Wal-Mart wasn't just under-pricing food staples or underwear. It was also figuring out how to bring its customers back into the parking lot more often. Expanding into groceries certainly did that — but gas stations fueled increased traffic as well. Once again, Wal-Mart found itself on the cheap side of a nasty court battle.

In March 2003, a federal judge in Oklahoma ordered Sam's Club to stop selling gas below cost. The court determined that Sam's club had lost $250,000 to $300,000 on gas sales at three stores in Oklahoma City, Oklahoma over an 8-month period. Oklahoma's Unfair Sales Act requires marketers to mark up gas sales at least 6% over "laid-in costs." It may be hard for consumers to appreciate why a state like Oklahoma would have a law regulating unfair sales. As with the German example, scrutiny over pricing was necessary to prevent long-term harm to the economy. For the consumer with an empty gas gauge, there may seem to be little rhyme or reason to pricing laws — but the concept is that if a company's pricing policy was established with the intent of driving competitors out of business by holding prices below wholesale cost, then consumers would ultimately pay the price.

The Oklahoma court case on gas prices indicated that Sam's Club's gross margin was less than .6%. The judge found Sam's Club testimony on the numbers was "contrived," and its pricing was "deceptive." The company's pricing policy had already caused a competitor to lose a large volume of its business. The court ruled that because Sam's was not a freestanding gas station, "the purpose of the gasoline business at these three stores is to pull customers in and to do so if need be by operating the gas facilities at a loss."

The Oklahoma Petroleum Marketers hailed the court decision as a "great victory for law-abiding marketers" in the state. "The court found that selling gasoline at a loss in order to lure customers to buy other merchandise is deceptive and impairs fair competition," the OPMA said.

When Wal-Mart and Sam's Clubs first opened up in Small Town, U.S.A., gas station operators told local officials they were optimistic that Wal-Mart would translate into more cars going by their front door. By the mid-1990s, however, when Wal-Mart started opening its own gas stations in its superstore parking lots, the oil marketers realized their mistake in not joining other businesses earlier to stop these megastores. They understood that for Wal-Mart, gas was just a loss leader to lure people into their stores, whereas for the gas dealer, petroleum was the blood in the veins of their business.

Germany, Wisconsin, Oklahoma — how many other places will spend the time and money to challenge Wal-Mart's effort to leverage its size and influence over the market to drive its competitors out of business? Federal anti-trust law is a legal thicket. It's not easy to prove a company's intent to harm others, and the sanctions are largely symbolic to a corporation with the resources of a Wal-Mart. What's a $175,000 fine to a company that had net sales in 2003 of $244 billion dollars?

In the fall of 2003 I received a call from a concrete supplier. He had just gotten off the phone with a big box retailer who had informed him that the retailer planned to sell bagged cement to the public at prices below their invoiced cost from the supplier — and he did not want the supplier to be shocked when he saw the pricing of his product. "I urged them not to do that," the supplier told me. "But they said: 'Hey, that's just how we operate.'" The concrete supplier knew that this pricing below cost was going to kill off his other customers, the local retailers who couldn't afford to sell below cost. If the other retailers died off, the supplier would become even more dependent on the one large big box customer, and then the pressure would build for the supplier to lower his wholesale price. The super-retailers, like Wal-Mart, are playing with a stacked deck, and they are using their customers as human shields to protect them from criticism. Wal-Mart customers demand low prices, and everything that Wal-Mart does to satisfy that demand is justified, because the "Customer Is Boss."

After decades of being told that Wal-Mart has the lowest prices, it is certain that most consumers believe it. But in Carroll County, Arkansas, the local newspaper decided to explore Wal-Mart's "low price" claim. The Carroll County News staff generated a list of 19 household items, and then went to six stores in Berryville, Eureka Springs, and Green Forest, Arkansas. The shopping survey was conducted over a one-month period so as not to give any one store an unfair advantage for the shopping day to coincide with a sale. The CCN staff said the results were surprising. Of the 19 items purchased, Wal-Mart was the cheapest for only 2 of the 19 items:

> Wal-Mart, which advertises itself as the everyday low price leader, "Always the low price on the brands you trust—Always," isn't necessarily so. The lowest register receipt total for the nine items was $12.91. The highest on the total — the most expensive on the nine items, was Wal-Mart, at $15.86. At least on these two shopping days, on these items chosen at random, Wal-Mart isn't necessarily the everyday low price leader . . . Consumers have to decide for themselves where they are getting the best value, but the results of the CCN survey indicate that where we think we're getting the best value might not necessarily be where the best value can be found.

The National Grocer's Association, which represents thousands of independent grocery stores, has complained for years that federal anti-trust laws have not been enforced, and that the large retail corporations are benefiting from an uneven playing field. NGA Senior Vice President Tom Wenning told his members at their 2001 Annual Conference:

> Independent retailers and wholesalers...have raised growing concern about the need for public policy representation on a host of issues, from zoning exemptions, tax abatements, below-cost selling, and assuring a level competitive playing field when Wal-Mart enters their communities. Increasingly, public policy makers are evaluating and assessing these value issues at the local, state and federal levels. On the national level this includes the harmful effects of increased market concentration on consumers. In local communities zoning boards are questioning the impact of Wal-Mart entering their communities.

The NGA charges that big box retailers have extracted special deals from their vendors and that such deals have not been made available to the smaller grocery stores. Such deals include special pricing for large customers like Wal-Mart, special packaging and promotional allowances, more lenient payment and credit terms, and better product availability. The NGA says that lack of federal enforcement of anti-trust laws has "contributed greatly to the rush to bigness and mergers, as megachains seek to gain greater buying leverage with suppliers...The ability of large power buyers to demand and receive special preferential treatment in any of these...areas that are not made available to competitors violates the law, and fuels the fire for power buyers to seek even more buying clout through mergers and acquisitions."

People in the retail industry see what companies like Wal-Mart are doing to "competition." But where it really matters, in the aisles of local stores, the only competition that matters is today's prices. Trying to make the case that Wal-Mart damages competition in the "long run" is a tough sell to consumers who are calculating their purchase on this week's paycheck. But the consolidation of selling power into fewer and fewer hands, has everything to do with the ultimate price of bananas. Despite a chorus of economists praising Wal-Mart for lifting our standard of living, the company has actually been doing considerable damage to our economy.

# Count 6:
# Questionable Banking Practices

*"Among other things, Walton Enterprises owns banks in several towns around here. Jim [Walton] and a partner own the local newspaper, the Daily Record."*

—Sam Walton, <u>Made in America</u>

Millions of Americans each week walk past a Wal-Mart greeter on their way to discount prices. Like a computer virus, the nation's largest private employer has spread from underwear, to groceries, to gasoline, to used cars, to travel services — all imprinted with the culture of founder Sam Walton.

Local merchants complain that when consumers spend local dollars at a Wal-Mart, that money is deposited into "sweep accounts" that are cleaned out each night and wired to Wal-Mart's central bank. Behind the discount store empire, there is another Walton empire where no greeters lurk. It is a secret empire largely unknown to the public. It is where the Wal-Mart dollars go.

On several occasions, Wal-Mart has attempted to break down what bankers call "the firewall" that separates retailers from banking. According to the Independent Community Banking Association (ICBA), which represents 5,000 community banks across the country, "the linchpin of the financial and economic system of the United States is the principle of separating banking and commerce...[which] prevents conflicts of interest and undue concentration of resources, and ensure the impartial allocation of credit..." Imagine a developer with a Kmart or Target project in hand going to a Wal-Mart bank for a loan. Or picture your Wal-Mart bank issuing a credit card that allows them to keep tabs on where you shop. In your monthly statement you might find a notice that says: "We notice you did your grocery shopping at Kroger this month. Did you see the great prices Wal-Mart had on deli items?"

In August 2003, independent bankers went to the press to warn that Wal-Mart was trying to set up an industrial loan corporation (ILC) that would be based in Utah. From that ILC, Wal-Mart could open branches in all of its stores nationwide. "If Wal-Mart is allowed to set up an ILC in Utah," said a spokesperson for the Independent Community Bankers of America (ICBA), "it would give the company an unbelievable amount of economic power." ILC's have been described as a "hybrid" type of financial institution. They operate like banks with federal deposit insurance; they can issue credit cards, put money on deposit, and issue loans. According to the Salt Lake Tribune, they can't offer standard checking accounts if they are holding assets over $100 million. Congress is still considering legislation that would make it easier for ILC's to branch out across state lines. When the ILC flap hit the press, a Wal-Mart spokesman said: "We don't own any banks, nor do we have any plans right now to get into that business beyond the services we already offer."

Wal-Mart's efforts to bust into banking by purchasing the Federal Bank Centre, a savings and loan in Broken Arrow, Oklahoma, or the Toronto-Dominion bank in Canada, encountered strong industry and regulatory opposition. But Wal-Mart's greatest penetration of the firewall between commerce and banking took place quietly 41 years ago in the small town of Bentonville, Arkansas, without a single objection.

The Bank of Bentonville opened its doors in 1931 on Bentonville Square. It stands today, one block from the Wal-Mart Museum that canonizes the career of Sam Walton, the pioneering discount retailer. But the Bank of Bentonville knew Sam Walton by another title — owner of the bank.

One year before he opened the first Wal-Mart in Rogers, Arkansas, Sam Walton became the owner of a majority interest in the Bank of Bentonville. Using a $350,000 loan from the Republic National Bank of Dallas, Texas, Sam Walton bought a bank. Between 1961 and the present, the Bank of Bentonville metastasized into the Arvest Bank Group, a network of banks in northeast and central Oklahoma, southwest Missouri, and northwest Arkansas. This banking network controls $4.7 billion worth of assets, and employs roughly 2,700 people. According to Bank News, the banking magazine of the central states, "Arvest Bank is an expansion of the Arvest Bank Group, owned by the Walton family from Wal-Mart fame. Since its inception, the company has grown to 12 different charters, including 45 banking locations."

Walton's banking empire grew by acquisitions, buying banks with homespun names like the Bank of Pea Ridge and the First National Bank of Siloam Springs. Like its discount chain, Wal-Mart's banking chain began in the familiar terrain of small town Arkansas. It bought the McElroy Bank & Trust in Fayetteville in 1986, and the Security National Bank of Norman, Oklahoma in 1987.

The Arvest banks today offer "full business and consumer services, including consumer and mortgage lending, deposit services, investment and trust services, retirement planning, employee benefit services, personalized employee banking packages, and business cash management." Consumers can also get a credit card through Arvest's Security National Bank. Arvest has been a federally chartered thrift institution since 1995. It also operates the Arvest Insurance Company & Trust Company, which sells life insurance and annuities. Arvest Asset Management is a subsidiary of Arvest Bank, which publishes *The Arvest 50*, a list of 50 public stocks, including Wal-Mart Stores, Inc. According to Bob Ortega, in his book *In Sam We Trust*, "the Bank of Bentonville...was serving as the trustee for various Wal-Mart benefit plans with enormous financial holdings."

At the center of this banking empire is Jim C. Walton, the chairman and CEO of Arvest Bank Group, and the third son of Sam Walton. Jim Walton was listed among the top ten richest persons in the world by *Forbes* magazine in 2003, and has served as head of Walton Enterprises. He is a major stockholder in Wal-Mart Stores, Inc. His financial worth was estimated at $21 billion. This is clearly someone with strong financial interest in the welfare of the Wal-Mart retail operation, sitting at the controls of a banking empire founded by his father. The retail/banking relationship is so incestuous, Arvest even has branches located inside a Wal-Mart supercenter. In Bentonville, for example, the supercenter at 406 South Walton Street has an Arvest bank branch store inside the Wal-Mart. So the "firewall" separating Wal-Mart from banking is fiction.

What's the problem with Wal-Mart controlling a banking empire? Bankers worry that Wal-Mart's involvement in both sectors presents the dangers of concentration of resources and impaired credit availability. The ICBA warns, "These dangers are amplified because of the company's known role in devastating the vitality of many small town centers."

What will happen to credit, the ICBA asks, if the Wal-Mart bank siphons deposits from locally-owned banks, weakening their ability to support local economic growth? Like storm water runoff from a Wal-Mart parking lot, will capital resources be drained away from hometowns? "Will a local hardware or clothing store, a local pharmacy, or someone wishing to establish a new store, be able to obtain credit from the Wal-Mart bank?" the ICBA asks. The banking industry sees Wal-Mart banks as being unable to make impartial credit decisions because of a conflict of interest.

For years, critics have complained that Wal-Mart stores export deposits out of local communities by putting its money into "sweep" accounts that are wired to Arkansas overnight, instead of remaining in local banks for community reinvestment. But virtually no attention has been paid to the conflicts inherent in the Arvest banking conglomerate, which Sam Walton quietly purchased in small town Arkansas, and then left in the hands of son number three.

Sam Walton probably assumed that if he owned a bank, his retailing business would never come up short if it needed a loan. But a giant Wal-Mart banking/retail conglomerate would give Wal-Mart unprecedented consolidation of power over both industries.

In the fall of 2003, Wal-Mart began a test program of providing Wal-Mart "Money Centers" inside 16 of its stores in Georgia and Tennessee. Wal-Mart says that one-fifth of its customers don't have checking accounts. The Wal-Mart "Money Centers" are actually owned by the Memphis-based National Bank of Commerce (NBC). The *Associated Press* reported that the co-branded Wal-Mart/NBC deal was for 2 years. NBC, which has 500 branches, has actually been inside Wal-Mart stores for more than a decade, but the new deal makes the bank look like it is owned by Wal-Mart, because the retailer's name is in much larger letters than the bank's. The bank said the emphasis on the Wal-Mart logo is to bring in customers who may not have much money now but will earn more later. "Wal-Mart obviously has a very well known and powerful brand," an NBC spokesman said. "If we can work with them to extend that to financial services, we're going to see if we can do that." One financial analyst commented on the Wal-Mart/NBC deal, suggesting that banks can make a profit on low-income customers by charging fees on individual transactions and service charges on bounced checks.

# Count 7:
# Exploiting Global Trade

*"One, two, three, four, kick those sweatshops out the door!*
*Five, six, seven, eight, workers need a living rate!"*
— Seventh graders marching in front of the Wal-Mart store in Janesville, Wisconsin,
December 14, 1999

NAFTA opened up what Wal-Mart has called its "one market" opportunities. As trade barriers dropped, international sales became perhaps the most important source of new sales for a company that in the early 1990s was eagerly looking to do more than increase its "same store sales." In 1994, Rob Walton, then Chairman of Wal-Mart stores, told his stockholders: "We're poised to explode onto the international market and transplant our terrific Wal-Mart way of doing business to other countries."

In 1994, Wal-Mart created its International Division. Wal-Mart had been in Mexico since 1991, and was in the process of expanding its Mexican operations with its Mexican partner, CIFRA, SA, opening its first two supercenters south of the border in 1994. "We are pleased with the sales at both locations," Wal-Mart told its stockholders. That same year, Wal-Mart announced its first "opportunistic acquisition" of 122 Woolco stores in Canada for $335 million.

With successes in Canada and Mexico under its belt, Wal-Mart told shareholders: "While we will proceed cautiously in light of obvious cultural differences, we are confident that the Wal-Mart concept is exportable."

A decade later, in Wal-Mart's 2003 Annual Report, there is a picture of a small child holding a globe in his hands. The international division had grown to nearly $41 billion in annual sales, or roughly 17% of the company's total sales of $244 billion. By comparison, in 1998, international sales were only 6% of the company's total sales. Between 1998 and 2003, Wal-Mart's overall sales doubled, from $118 billion to $244 billion, but during the same time period, international sales increased more than five-fold.

"For perspective," wrote Wal-Mart CEO Lee Scott, "if Wal-Mart International were a stand-alone company, it would rank number 33 on last year's *Fortune* 500 list based on sales." Measured by sales, the international stores had become Wal-Mart's second largest division, second only to its U.S. Wal-Mart stores division.

At the close of its 2003 fiscal year, Wal-Mart had stores in Canada, Argentina, Brazil, Mexico and Puerto Rico; European stores in Britain and Germany; and Asian stores in Korea and China. The international division had 942 discount stores, 238 supercenters and 71 Sam's Clubs. Most of this growth was accomplished by buying out existing companies, like ASDA in Britain, Amigos in Puerto Rico and Bodegas and Vips in Mexico.

As if damage to the U.S. economy from Wal-Mart's displacement of smaller companies was not bad enough, the concept is now being exported around the world. "Country by country," said the president of Wal-Mart's international division, "the world is discovering the great value of shopping at Wal-Mart."

But what the world soon discovered was that Wal-Mart's corporate strength was built on the backs of everyday low-cost labor, and workers in the sweatshops of third world nations. Wal-Mart could create a colonial empire without storming a single capitol building, without leading a single political revolution. It didn't even have to own the sweatshops or the workers. It was an immaculate form of economic colonialism, coordinated from a nondescript little town in Arkansas.

Very few Americans ever get to Saipan, just north of Guam, one of the Northern Marianas floating in the Pacific Ocean. But your clothing has been there. Perhaps you have seen "Made in Northern Marianas" stitched into the label of your shirts.

In Saipan, where warm ocean breezes blow, thousands of destitute Asian women work like indentured slaves to produce the clothes sold at The Gap and Wal-Mart.

According to a series of class action lawsuits filed in 1999 in San Francisco, women workers assembling "Made in the USA" clothing are toiling in "hotbox" factories, suffering physical abuse from their supervisors, including forced abortions, and living in barbed-wire compounds infested by rats.

The San Francisco Chronicle reported that the lawsuits allege that as many as 25,000 Asian "guest workers" have suffered violations of labor, racketeering, human rights and business laws in Saipan. Besides Wal-Mart, other companies implicated in the lawsuit include Nordstrom, The Gap, Tommy Hilfiger, May Co., Sears and others.

Most remarkable of all: this is taking place in a U.S. Commonwealth. Saipan has been part of the U.S. for the past 24 years. As such, the island enjoys favorable U.S. tariff and duty protections, similar to those found in the Caribbean Basin Initiative. These sweatshops, which have been labeled "America's worst sweatshops," are given preferential tax treatment by the U.S. taxpayers.

The women employed in these factories come from China, the Philippines, Bangladesh and Thailand. They are lured to Saipan with the promise of good wages and fair working conditions. What they find instead are seven-day workweeks, 12-hour shifts, no overtime, substandard living conditions and barracks with lockdowns and curfews. Many workers reportedly can't return home because they would have to repay a $7,000 recruitment fee.

"Indentured servitude is alive and well in many parts of the world, including the United States," said one lawyer for the workers. The lawsuit was brought by the Union of Needletrades Industrial and Textile Employees (UNITE), and three California-based non-profits: Global Exchange, The Asian Law Caucus, and Sweatshop Watch.

The sweat of Saipan labor soaks the clothes with labels from the North Marianas Islands. Lawyers in this class action suit claim that big retailers have avoided more than $200 million in tariffs by having clothes made in Saipan. That's a form of corporate welfare that the rest of us pay for. Companies like Wal-Mart make millions in profits from marked up goods made for next to nothing by indentured Asian women.

But young women and children were not the only links in Wal-Mart's chain of worker exploitation. Similar pain and suffering was taking place much closer to home. Wal-Mart's appetite for foreign goods has turned life upside down in Kannapolis, North Carolina.

It must have been tough for Michael Gannaway to draft a letter that he knew would seem like the end of the world to nearly 6,500 families. "There is no easy way to communicate the disappointment and sadness," Gannaway wrote, "that surrounds our need to close the doors to a company with a proud and distinguished name."

Gannaway's letter silenced the massive looms of Kannapolis,

North Carolina. Here was the chairman and CEO of a 120-year-old business throwing in the towel. Literally. His Pillowtex Corporation, manufacturer of sheets and towels — such major brands as Fieldcrest, Royal Velvet and Cannon — shut down its 16 textile plants and dismissed 6,450 workers in the summer of 2003.

In the halcyon days of Pillowtex, the company's success had often been referred to by corporate officials as "A Bedtime Story." But in recent years, the bedtime tale turned instead into a nightmare.

Michael Gannaway's letter fell like a giant shroud over Kannapolis and its noiseless factories. Kannapolis, which means "city of looms," became the center of the largest permanent layoff in North Carolina history. The misery spread throughout Rowan, Rockingham and Cabarrus counties. Many small towns in North Carolina had grown up around the mills, and income from the mills was all that kept the towns financially solvent. Like the fabric on its looms, Pillowtex communities were woven together by economic dependency. The closing of Pillowtex meant that the Henry County school system lost $622,000 in revenues from its budget. That's on top of the $1.5 million in cuts earlier in 2003. What killed Pillowtex also cost teachers their jobs in Henry County.

"Our management team and employees have made extraordinary contributions as we attempted to avoid this unfortunate outcome," Gannaway wrote. "In the end we are faced with our worst-case scenario. I want to personally thank each Pillowtex employee for years of loyalty and service, and assure you that this decision was not reached lightly and without deep regret...This has been a challenging year for all of us. Each individual employee is a part of this company's great history, and it is profoundly sad to witness the end of its operations."

Gannaway called city officials and the union into his office in late July 2003 to give them the bad news. The announcement surely could not have come as a total surprise, since Pillowtex fabric had started to unravel at least three years earlier. The company went into Chapter 11 bankruptcy protection in November 2000 with more than $1 billion in debt. It emerged in May 2002 still carrying more than $200 million in debt, and went on to lose $27 million in the first seven months of its re-emergence. During its first bankruptcy, Pillowtex dumped 4,000 workers. The Bank of America had given the company extensions on a $150 million loan five times. It was also obvious on the production floor that the company was in deep straits: most plants had been idle for over a month, as Pillowtex turned to its inventories to complete what orders it had, rather than make more products. Some workers had been on furlough for two months.

There were a few false hopes raised before the company slipped into oblivion. In June 2003 there was news that a British company, Homestead Fabrics, might buy Pillowtex. But creditors apparently didn't find the offer suitable, and the deal unraveled. There were other suitors too — like WestPoint Stevens and Springs Industries — but these companies had their own financial problems with which to contend.

A few days after the official announcement that Pillowtex would close, North Carolina Governor Michael F. Easley wrote a letter of his own. His was sent to President George W. Bush. Easley sent the President video footage of several Pillowtex workers who had lost their jobs. "I heard their stories when I visited the plant in May," the Governor wrote, "and I wanted you to have the same opportunity to hear directly from them on this important issue."

Easley's pitch to President Bush was that these workers "have given much of their life to ensure that 'Made in America' is synonymous with a high quality product. Many of their children are defending our freedom overseas. These families desperately need the help of your administration." Easley blamed the federal government for Pillowtex's demise, and called on the Bush Administration to rescind trade agreements and to enact protections for U.S. manufacturers.

But what caused such a venerable company — the second largest maker of towels in the country, which had survived 12 decades of good times and lean times — to suddenly come undone? Some observers blamed it on the company's computer system, which could not track sales, and left the company overstocked with inventories. Wall Street analysts said that the company had trouble servicing its debt "as it struggles with heavy competition from cheap imports in the depressed textile industry."

From the outside, Pillowtex's customers seemed strong enough: some of its main accounts were with retailers like Wal-Mart, Kohl's and Kmart. But a foreshadowing of the outcome came in August 2000, when Kmart announced that it would no longer buy Pillowtex towels. The retailer would not give specifics at the time, but a spokesperson said that Kmart had "stopped doing the towel business with Pillowtex...September 14 is the date the last towel order will be placed with them." At the time, Pillowtex had sales of $1.6 billion. A spokesperson for Wachovia Securities downplayed the event. "Was this a huge piece of Pillowtex's business? I doubt it," the analyst said. "Pillowtex does $1.6 billion in business annually, so a towel program at one retailer isn't going to make or break them." But by 2002, sales had fallen to below $1 billion, and the "make" was turning rapidly into "break." Pillowtex was losing more than just one "towel program."

Some critics of the company showed little mercy. "Pillowtex was neither the canary in the coal mine nor the last man standing in the American textile industry," wrote Bill Mann of the financial analyst website, The Motley Fool. "It is but another casualty in a dying industry." According to Mann, the downfall of Pillowtex was inevitable. "The reality is that Pillowtex, like many of its brethren, could not earn enough to cover the expense of keeping its American mills open, for the simple reason that the price points where consumers demand their products are a tool for these companies to retain operations in the United States. They cannot compete with foreign mills, where expenses are substantially less." The ugly truth, according to Mann, is that "the American textile industry is in decline because it is an unsustainable business when dependent upon high-cost American labor...Pillowtex's attempt to keep its manufacturing in the U.S. came at the price of every penny of shareholder's money."

It is certainly true that North Carolina has been hard hit by the shift from manufacturing to a retail economy. Between 2000 and 2003, more than 3,500 workers in northwest North Carolina lost their jobs. Textiles and furniture were the big losers. One woman told the Wall Street Journal: "As people are laid off and have to take a job with less pay, they're forced to spend as little as possible for what they need, which leads them directly to — what else — imports."

Michael Gannaway's letter to his workers laid it out clearly: lagging sales and a flood of cheap imports combined to snap the towel:

> The textile industry is facing unprecedented increases in global manufacturing capacity combined with softening demand in a tough retail environment. For well over two decades, the U.S. textile industry has been under constant pressure to reorganize while facing fierce competition from overseas manufacturers. Cheap imports are flooding the U.S. market and driving down prices, while global sourcing has created a new business model for textile companies that we are unable to replicate without substantial investments. These trends are being seen nationwide, and have created a marketplace

where we can no longer offer our customers the merchandise they need at prices that are profitable for this company.

In 2002, according to Morningstar, an investment research firm, Wal-Mart accounted for 28% of Pillowtex's revenue. Pillowtex's survival was perilously dependent on companies like Wal-Mart, who were aggressively stepping up their purchase of cheaper Chinese products just at the time that Pillowtex sales were coming apart at the seams. Wal-Mart's drive to mark down prices helped to make American labor unaffordable at companies like Pillowtex. The only comment Wal-Mart made in the wake of Pillowtex's fall was short, and ironically designed to bolster Wal-Mart's "Made in America" image. "We were surprised and saddened by the news," Wal-Mart spokesman Tom Williams said, adding, "The majority of the outstanding orders at Pillowtex have been sent to other suppliers in the U.S." The largest importer of Chinese apparel in the world was surprised and saddened by the loss of one of its U.S. suppliers. But clearly Wal-Mart orders were not enough to keep Pillowtex in business, and the company went under in the flood of cheap Chinese goods that companies like Wal-Mart helped create.

North Carolina Congressman Richard Burr says he voted against giving China normal trade relations in 2000, because he saw what the future would bring. "It was clear even then that China's subsidized, sweatshop manufacturing would devour domestic industry — particularly textiles and furniture. The blame for the millions of manufacturing jobs lost in the United States over the past three years can, I believe, be traced in part to those votes in the House and Senate in 2000 that granted those trade relations to China."

The economists could debate which was dropping faster—consumer prices or worker's wages—but none of that was of much consolation to the former workers at Pillowtex. According to state figures, the average age of Pillowtex employees was 46.3 years. About 27% of them were over the age of 55, and the typical worker had been with the company for more than 13 years. The average annual wage of hourly workers was $22,610 a year. The hourly wage averaged around $11. State officials say that if these workers find new jobs, they are likely to bring home smaller paychecks than they did at the looms. Such displaced workers frequently have to take pay cuts of 55% to 60% at a new job.

When James Kyles, who worked at Pillowtex for nearly 40 years, heard the end was coming, he and his wife drove to Pillowtex headquarters to find out directly what was going on. "I'm 61 years old," he told the *Charlotte Observer*. "Where am I going to go to find a job? I've worked in the mill my whole life. I'm uneducated." His wife added: "People don't understand. All of these people with no education, where are they going to go?"

The answer seems painfully obvious. If James Kyles goes out into the job market, he is likely to find that many of the job openings in North Carolina are at retail stores like Wal-Mart. According to one newspaper account: "Several of Pillowtex's mills had closed in the past few years, leaving the area littered with the unemployed. A few got jobs at the Wal-Mart that went up at the edge of town."

If Chinese imports silenced the looms in Kannapolis, what happened to Sam Walton's "Made in America" pledge? Without any announcement from Bentonville, Wal-Mart began exhibiting its taste for Chinese take-out. For about a ten-year period beginning in 1985, Wal-Mart touted its "Buy American" program. In 1994, the company pledged that it was "constantly seeking more items to convert from foreign sources to American manufacturers. We prefer to place American-made products on our shelves. Millions of dollars in goods once produced overseas have been brought back to the USA. Thousands of American jobs have been created or retained because of this merchandising program."

But in the following decade, Wal-Mart's merchandising program no longer spoke English, as American products were substituted with foreign-made products at an astounding pace. In 1999, the National Labor Committee announced:

> The truth is, Wal-Mart has moved far more production offshore than the industry average. For example, only 11% of Wal-Mart's famous Kathie Lee line of clothing is made in the U.S., while 89% is made off-shore. Only 17% of Wal-Mart's men's Faded Glory clothing is made in the U.S., while 96% of its children's McKids label is made offshore. Wal-Mart has shifted the majority of its Kathie Lee production to Mexico and Indonesia — two countries where the local currencies collapsed, driving real wages through the floor, to 50¢ an hour in Mexico, and 9¢ in Indonesia. It is as if Wal-Mart were chasing misery.

Despite the megastore claims that they are "bringing it back to the USA," our American apparel industry has literally lost its shirt. According to a July 1998 report by the U.S. General Accounting Office, over the past 23 years, U.S. apparel industry jobs have shrunk by 41%, a staggering loss of 597,000 American jobs. There were 1,450,000 U.S. apparel workers in 1973, and only 853,000 similar jobs by 1996. According to the GAO, in 1995, more than half of the $178 billion in apparel sold at the retail level in the U.S. at companies like Wal-Mart was imported. Between 1987 and 1997, imports from the Caribbean grew from $864 million to $6.4 billion — a sevenfold increase.

In Bangladesh, 1,000 young workers at the Beximco plant in the Dhaka Export Processing Zone sew shirts and pants that are made for Wal-Mart and other retailers. According to the National Labor Committee, these workers often work 12 hours a day, seven days a week, or an 80-hour work week. They are sometimes forced to work a 24-hour shift straight through the night. They are paid less than one-third of the country's legal overtime rate. Although the official work week in Bangladesh is 48 hours plus a limit of 12 hours overtime, these workers are way over the legal boundary.

In 1998, goods shipped from this "export processing zone" rose by 56% to $186 million. Labor is very cheap, and there is a state guarantee of no unions. The South Koreans and Japanese often own these factories employing Bangladesh workers. Wal-Mart workers who sew clothes make 20 cents an hour, says the NLC, even though the official legal wage is 33 cents an hour. Helpers who work with the sewers only get 9 cents an hour. These companies working under Wal-Mart contracts give their workers no maternity leave, no health coverage, and even restrict their access to bathrooms. Although Wal-Mart says it has a "code of conduct" for its vendors, none of the workers in Beximco have seen the code, and none was posted at the workplace. To top it off, Wal-Mart pays no taxes to sew their clothes in the Export Processing Zone. Wal-Mart pays nothing in tariffs, even though Bangladesh is one of the poorest countries in the world.

According to an article on May 21, 2000 in *The New York Times*, Wal-Mart "already gets 53% of its clothing imports from China" based on U.S. customs documents, and the company admits to sourcing its products from "several thousand factories" in China.

Wal-Mart is America's largest importer of Chinese goods. The replacement of domestic products with imported goods has had an indelible effect on our economy. In June 2003, our trade deficit swelled to a record setting $136 billion in the first three months of the year. The U.S. Commerce Department said the trade deficit was nearly 6% higher than the previous record deficit set in the last quarter of 2002. As a direct result of Wal-Mart's foreign outsourcing, imported goods outpaced exports, illustrating that free trade has led to the flooding of the U.S. with cheap foreign products. Behind those cheap Chinese goods on Wal-Mart shelves are the millions of American manufacturing jobs that were exported to developing nations.

The United States currently imports 6.5 times as much from China as we export, and companies like Wal-Mart are in the forefront of this imbalance. We imported nearly $12 billion in toys, games and sporting goods from China in 1999, and $8.4 billion in shoes and sneakers alone. Another $7.3 billion was spent on clothing. Just as Congress has liberalized trade with China, new reports indicate that many of the factories American companies contract with in China are paying their workers wages as low as 3 cents an hour, working their employees 98-hour workweeks, requiring compulsory unpaid overtime, and banning talking during work hours. Wal-Mart is always prominently named as a company that sources its goods from such sweatshops. Based on import volume, Wal-Mart is more appropriately called "Shanghai-Mart."

Despite the U.S. Commerce Department's warning of the continually mushrooming trade deficit with China, Wal-Mart imports continually rise. China bought 3% of U.S. exports in 2002, but provided 11% of our imports. Trade with China accounted for nearly 22% of the U.S. merchandise trade deficit in 2002. The discount giants will argue that flooding America with cheap goods keeps prices down, and encourages consumers to spend money. But over-dependence on imports has its dangerous side, too. "When trade becomes too one-sided," warns the National Association of Manufacturers (NAM), "it can slow economic growth."

In the first quarter of 2003, the overall U.S. trade deficit was a record $136.1 billion — or almost $545 billion a year. By comparison, Wal-Mart sales in 2003 were $244 billion. The *Associated Press* wrote, "U.S. companies have moved operations overseas, while imports flood into the United States, a combination that has cost millions of lost American manufacturing jobs." In fact, since 2000, American manufacturing has lost 2 million jobs, or four times the loss in the preceding decade. Manufacturing jobs as a percentage of total employment fell from 13.2% in 2000 to 11.4% in early 2003, according to the NAM. A NAM study of manufacturing losses concluded, "The movement overseas of manufacturers affects the entire industrial network. As manufacturers relocated overseas, suppliers all the way up the supply chain must make plans to relocate as well." On average each year between 1993 and 1998, 177,000 American manufacturing workers with three or more years of experience lost their jobs — and between January 1999 and December 2001 the Bureau of Labor Statistics says the job loss rate increased to 230,000 workers each year. In June 2003, 56,000 manufacturing jobs were lost. The two lowest paid sectors of our economy — retail and services — rose from 30% of the job market in 1965 to 48% of the market by 1998. We have about twice as many cashiers in America as we do software engineers. Roughly one in four workers in this country earn less than $9 an hour.

In April 2000, *Site Selection* magazine listed as its "incentives deal of the month" the construction of a 1 million-square-foot Wal-Mart import distribution center in Virginia, near the line between James City County and the city of Newport News. This facility helped Wal-Mart bring to our shores all those consumer goods that used to be manufactured in the U.S., but are now stamped "Made in China." Wal-Mart imported so many millions of tons of foreign goods that it needed a larger distribution center to handle the stuff. If Wal-Mart was a country, it would be China's eighth largest export destination.

According to *Site Selection*, Virginia had been quietly wooing Wal-Mart with more than just the wonderful attributes of the region. James River set up a 2,400 acre "Enterprise Zone" and gave Wal-Mart a $950,000 grant over a six-year period. Wal-Mart took up 200 acres in the Green Mount Industrial Park, and got nearly $1 million in corporate welfare for doing so. But there's more. The state of Virginia also tossed in a $700,000 grant from the Virginia Governor's Opportunity Fund. The total incentive package "hasn't been disclosed" the magazine said, but it also included road improvements along Route 60 paid for by taxpayers. Wal-Mart claimed that the import facility would initially employ 230 people, and the company expects it to double in size to 2 million square feet, adding another 170 jobs — even as more U.S. production facilities close.

The state of Virginia might as well have kept its wallet out, because over time those roadways are going to need continuing upgrades, considering that 54,750 truck trips, loaded down with Chinese goods, will rumble over those asphalt lanes annually. The import center opened for Chinese goods by December 2000, thanks to $1.65 million in grants, plus free roadwork. Taxpayers continue to subsidize the operations of corporations like Wal-Mart, while American manufacturing of retail goods shifts to foreign countries, and our trade deficit balloons to new heights. According to an October 28, 2003 *Marketplace* broadcast, the United States imports $125 billion in Chinese goods, and Wal-Mart alone is responsible for $12 billion of that total.

Sam Walton admitted that his company at one time had fallen into "a pattern of knee-jerk import buying, without really examining possible alternatives." In 1997, members of the Professional Workers Association picketed a Wal-Mart store in Newburgh, New York after 290 workers were laid off at the Hudson Valley Tree Company. Wal-Mart had canceled its contract with the artificial Christmas tree manufacturer. Hudson Valley Tree claims it lost its contract with Wal-Mart because the retailer found a similar product in China. A Wal-Mart representative said the company purchased 83% of its trees from a Virginia-based company and 17% from China.

In 1996, the Kanienkeha Lure Company, owned by the native American Mohawks, went out of business on the St. Regis Mohawk Reservation in northern New York state when Wal-Mart decided to pull their contract for fishing lures. 80 workers at the Kanienkeha factory lost their jobs, and the Mohawks urged a boycott of the chain.

According to research by *Wall Street Journal* reporter Bob Ortega, Wal-Mart's highly publicized "Buy American" program had little impact on the company's import activity:

> By 1988, Walton was saying that Wal-Mart had brought back to U.S. manufacturers $1.2 billion in retail goods . . . creating or saving some 17,000 jobs. But Wal-Mart's direct imports, as a percentage of sales, hadn't shrunk at all, because the company was buying more goods directly than before — including more imported goods. Wal-Mart's buying staff in Hong Kong and Taipei alone had grown to 90 people.

In 2003, Wal-Mart announced it had opened a procurement export center in Shanghai to buy merchandise in Northern and Eastern China. According to *Chain Store Age*, Wal-Mart imported more than $10 billion in goods from China last year. Wal-Mart also has a partnership with China International Trust and Investment to develop supermarkets in the general Shanghai region. As of 2003, Wal-Mart had 26 stores in China.

The "Shanghai-Mart" phenomenon has resulted in a lowering of the value of labor in America, and the fostering of sweatshops in foreign countries. Retailer reliance on imports has substantially eroded our domestic manufacturing jobs and output, resulting in workers with less discretionary income to spend in the American marketplace, and an economy more dependent on cashiers and stockboys. Consultant Ken Stone, who advises local businesses how to survive Wal-Mart, says damage has been done. "The thing I'm most concerned about," Stone told a reporter in Jackson, Michigan, "is that because they are so big, they can force prices down from their suppliers. There's a ripple effect that goes on and on. Almost all of [Wal-Mart's] apparel is made in China. Same in hardware. We're losing good manufacturing jobs in this country."

America exports high-tech merchandise to China, and imports cheap consumer goods. We send China airplanes, industrial machinery and telecommunications equipment, and we import shoes, toys and clothing. The labor movement in America has argued that when we buy Wal-Mart goods made in China, we are lowering the value of labor in America, and encouraging sweatshops in foreign countries. Wal-Mart's shopping pattern has exacerbated our nation's balance of trade deficit. The bumper sticker that once read: "Think locally, act globally," should be replaced with the new sprawl sticker: "Profit locally, buy globally."

"The confusion about our Buy American program," former Wal-Mart CEO David Glass told a Town Hall Forum in St. Louis in 1993, "is we've never said that we buy everything in America." In the summer of 2003, when Wal-Mart opened its first store in Beijing, China, many of the "American" products on the shelves were actually made inside China. The Heinz baby food was produced in Guangzhou. The Budweiser beer was not brewed in St. Louis, it came from Wuhan. The Tang powdered drink came from Tianjin.

Manufacturing jobs that started in New England, migrated to North Carolina, then traveled to Mexico, and then to China—always seeking the lowest wage levels on the planet. Chinese imports have hurt the Mexican economy by replacing Mexican sweatshops and Mexican retail products. A representative of the Grupo Textil Providencia in Mexico told The *Boston Globe* in November 2003 that Chinese goods were entering the United States, where tariffs are low, being illegally re-tagged "Made in the USA," and then imported into Mexico tax-free under NAFTA rules. "We can compete if the playing field is even. But it's not," he complained. Roughly 80,000 Mexican textile workers have lost their jobs since 2000. Even worse, the Mexican government estimated that 230,000 jobs have been lost in the same time period in the maquiladora sweatshops along the U.S. border, as 500 Mexican assembly plants (14% of the total plants) shut down and moved to China. Workers in China get paid half of what Mexican workers receive, and factory utility costs are lower. Overall, China is projected to become America's second largest trading partner after Canada, knocking Mexico down to third place. NAFTA put wheels under manufacturing jobs — moving them out of the United States to Central America and Mexico — and ultimately to Asia.

The Wal-Mart "Made in the USA" campaign began in 1985, and lasted for about a decade. From a 2003 perspective, looking back on the 1994 Wal-Mart employee's handbook, the company's commitment to U.S. products seems almost quaint and archival:

> We are constantly seeking more items to convert from foreign sources to American manufacturers. We prefer to place American-made products on our shelves.
>
> It's important to know that this program is not an anti-import campaign. It does not promote or suggest trade regulations, tariffs or controls on imported items. And it is not a subsidy program for American companies or workers. It does not guarantee an outlet for goods of inferior quality or higher price than foreign-made goods. It is not a blind commitment to buy American products at any price.

In one of the most dramatic policy reversals in retail history, Wal-Mart threw open its arms to Chinese goods, in a blind commitment to importing the very products that once were proudly labeled "Made in the U.S.A." By so doing, the company poked a great big hole in the American manufacturing lunch box.

# Count 8:
# Corporate Welfare Abuse

*"The city can't afford to be giving away money to the world's richest corporation. That's corporate welfare."*

— Attorney David Donaldson, Birmingham, Alabama lawsuit, September 2003

Former President Bill Clinton promised to end "welfare as we know it." He made no promises about ending corporate welfare as we know it. Yet public subsidies for corporations are the financial foundation that support the entire superstructure of exploitation that now threatens to monopolize the retail marketplace as we know it.

Wal-Mart is the richest company ever to get on welfare. It uses tax dollars to gain unfair advantage over its competitors, and to build new stores that shut down older ones.

In the winter of 2003, the state of Alabama had 34 Wal-Mart discount stores that were open and 15 that were closed. The state had a total of 1.2 million square feet of "dark stores" on the market. Most of these properties were closed to make way for larger superstores nearby.

Wal-Mart announced in 2002 that it wanted to replace an "aging" company discount store in Huffman. According to the *Birmingham News,* city officials in Birmingham promptly offered to give Wal-Mart $10 million in corporate welfare by refunding sales taxes to the company as an enticement to build a supercenter locally. Under the deal, the city would give Wal-Mart a 90% refund of the sales tax for roughly the first five years of the store's sales. With sales expected to be around $2.2 million a year, it would take just under 5 years to reach $10 million, at which point, the city would begin to receive its first dollar in sales tax. Birmingham officials defended the give-back deal by pointing out that Wal-Mart would "create"

250 jobs. But a local merchant and resident filed a lawsuit in September 2003 to prevent the city from honoring this blatant corporate free lunch. Southeastern Meats of Pelham, Inc. and William Craig charged in Jefferson County Court that Birmingham officials were giving Wal-Mart an unfair advantage over its smaller competitors, misusing tax dollars and unfairly using eminent domain powers to coerce landowners to sell their land to the Wal-Mart development.

Southeastern Meats has operated a store near the proposed Wal-Mart site for more than two decades. The company complained that the city never offered *them* any tax incentives to stay. "Southeastern Meats is standing up for all other small businesses that will be hurt by this new Wal-Mart," the merchant's attorney said. The lawsuit said that the tax break was just a fancy giveaway that would redistribute the tax money already being collected, with money formerly spent at smaller merchants in Birmingham now going to Wal-Mart. "The city's $10 million gift to Wal-Mart cannot be justified on the grounds that it will generate new jobs or additional tax revenue," the suit said. "The city's gift was irrelevant to Wal-Mart's business decision to replace its Wal-Mart stores with supercenters. The Huffman Wal-Mart would have been replaced with a supercenter regardless of the city's $10 million gift."

The law firm handling the lawsuit told the *News* that "with possible schoolteacher layoffs due to the funding crisis and police suing over not being paid overtime, the city cannot afford to be giving away money to the world's richest corporation. That's corporate welfare." The lawsuit also took issue with the city's threat to take properties by eminent domain, which gave Wal-Mart "an unfair and unlawful advantage over its competitors. By using the threat of eminent domain, Wal-Mart was able to coerce the landowners and tenants of the coveted parcel to sell the land to Wal-Mart for less than it could have been obtained on the open market." The lawsuit claimed that eminent domain was supposed to be used for public developments — like roads and schools — not for private gain.

A couple of months earlier, Mayor Dwight Welch of Country Club Hills, Illinois made a similar pact with Wal-Mart. The Mayor promised Wal-Mart that if they built a 200,000-square-foot supercenter in the city, the corporation would get half of its property taxes and sale taxes abated for the next decade. The sales tax abatement alone would provide Wal-

Mart with a $3 million subsidy — this for a company that had $8 billion in profits last year.

"We've got to get something going, and Wal-Mart will be our salvation," the Mayor told reporters. The next day's headline in the *Daily Southtown* read: "Wal-Mart Hinges Deal on Rebates." Most Wal-Mart shoppers expect the retailer to offer the rebates, but it actually works the other way around.

Corporate welfare is just one of the many ways that Wal-Mart manages to bring everyday low prices to the consumer. The world's largest retailer depends on welfare to perform its trade, and has given a deeper meaning to the phrase "free market."

One of the most generous states for corporate welfare is the Empire State. New York has been willing to spread tax dollars liberally to attract the wealthiest retailer in the world. New York Governor George Pataki himself showed up with his entourage in Johnstown, New York one September morning in 1998 to sign over tax money to Wal-Mart.

As he stood in front of all the state and local officials, Pataki drove the point home. "This development," he said, "is another sign that New York's economy has turned the corner."

Pataki proceeded to hand a large amount of state taxpayer's dollars over to the largest retail corporation in the world, with [at the time] $46 billion assets and 3,408 stores. A Wal-Mart regional food distribution center was born.

What "turned the corner" in Pataki's mind was the use of local and state tax subsidies for a company that had already turned the corner on $122 billion in sales, and could easily have paved its way from Bentonville, Arkansas to Johnstown, New York — and back again. New York taxpayers laid at Wal-Mart's feet an impressive assortment of gifts:

- a $650,000 capital grant
- a $250,000 employee training grant
- up to $1 million in roadway improvements
- sales tax abatements and funding for water and facility improvements provided gratis by the Fulton County Industrial Development Agency

The Chairman of the Empire State Development Corporation

said this heavily subsidized project was "just another example of how Governor Pataki's economic policies are creating jobs and opportunities for New Yorkers." But there was nobody from accounting to point out that many of the 400 "permanent full-time jobs" at the new warehouse would be offset by job losses at regional grocery stores, which would lose market share to Wal-Mart, close facilities and lay off workers.

There would be no oversized foamboard checks, no politicians in long overcoats around when those other stores "turned the corner" into Chapter 11, or shut down their warehouse facilities. The fact is, Wal-Mart's move into groceries has been accompanied by a significant negative economic impact on other area businesses. A more honest appraisal of the Johnstown Wal-Mart project is that it was a form of economic displacement — not a form of economic development. The use of tax dollars to subsidize the opening of a private warehouse that would put other warehouses and suppliers out of business was surely a strange way for the Empire State to help the Walton Empire to turn the corner.

The taxpayers of New York State — including many small merchants — were underwriting costs for the world's richest retailer, helping them gain another share of the "free market" they already dominate.

Another illustration of how public money has been used for private gain also comes from New York's Empire Zone. The very name sounds like something from a George Lucas movie, but it's actually a real place in the universe where large corporations go to receive massive state tax breaks used to destroy their competitors. It's the home of welfare for corporations, in this case nestled in the Hudson Valley of New York. Companies like Wal-Mart and Target, with the complicity of state and local officials, hide their presence under code names like "Project Mars" (Target) or "Project Competition" (Wal-Mart) to make sure the taxpayers who are going to subsidize these monstrosities don't have the faintest idea who they are nurturing.

Wal-Mart announced its distribution center around the same time as Target. Both corporations were depending on taxpayer's welfare in the Empire Zone to help underwrite their stores, in essence making some of their competitors pay for property, sales and payroll tax subsidies, in order to put them out of business. Empire Zone status meant a business could operate on an almost tax-free basis for up to 10 years. In the EZ, businesses can reap:

- A refundable credit against state business tax equal to a percentage of property taxes paid, based on the number of jobs created in the zone.
- A wage-tax credit for up to five years of $1,500 to $3,000 per year for each full-time job created.
- A sales tax rebate on purchases of building materials used in construction within the zone.
- A 10-year exemption from state sales tax on purchases of goods and services used mainly in the zone.

These tax breaks can add up to tens of millions of dollars for a million-foot warehouse. All these tax breaks are squeezed into a 2-square-mile area known as the Empire Zone.

Wal-Mart had intimated that if it didn't get the taxpayer's handout as part of the Empire Zone, it might not build. "If it were to get to that point," a Wal-Mart spokesman said, "it's something we'd have to consider in terms of how it would impact the project."

One member of the Orange County legislature, Thomas Pahucki, referred to the Empire Zone as "a corporate welfare roll that the people of New York would have to support."

In early August 2002, the *Times Herald* newspaper reported officially what many residents of Orange county knew for months. Target had settled on a site next to the Orange County Airport on 200 acres in the town of Montgomery, to build a 1.6 million-square-foot distribution center, which local officials — sworn to secrecy — referred to only by its code name, "Project Mars." At the same time, a second 1.2 million-square-foot Wal-Mart distribution center, code named "Project Competition," was proposed in the Town of Wallkill.

All these lucrative public subsidies made the Empire Zone resemble a duty-free state liquor store. But similar welfare plans for big retail corporations were being approved all over the country.

In the spring of 1999, Wal-Mart engineers surveyed a 193-acre parcel of land in Tomah, Wisconsin destined to become its next food distribution center. The company proposed the construction of an 880,000-square-foot grocery distribution center that would serve as the supply link to its future supercenter expansion into Wisconsin, Illinois and Iowa. The Tomah site is at the intersection of two major interstate highways. This distribution center would serve as the brain center to synchronize the movement of grocery products to several hundred Wal-Mart supercenters in the Midwest.

The taxpayers of Tomah bought the land for $2.4 million, then sold it to Wal-Mart for only $775,000 — less than one-third of its purchase price. The city also agreed to use its influence to get state and federal officials to build an interchange onto Interstate 94, gifting Wal-Mart with a $5 million road improvement.

The city even agreed to provide temporary city office space to Wal-Mart so it could begin interviewing job candidates. The city planned to make back some of the cost of infrastructure work at the site through a tax increment financing scheme. All these financing deals wrote down the project cost to Wal-Mart — a company that had $137 billion in sales at the time of this transaction.

The owners of small grocery stores in Illinois, Wisconsin and Iowa watched from the sidelines as one giant retailer got corporate welfare that ultimately would be used to put them out of business. They didn't want to speak out against the workings of the free market — but they never imagined the "free" market meant multi-million-dollar handouts to their wealthiest rival.

The same story unfolded in Lewiston, Maine. The ground was frozen solid in February 2002 when Wal-Mart and public officials announced the construction of a new 900,000-square-foot distribution center. City officials had negotiated with the corporation for more than six months in secret before the deal went public. Just before Christmas 2001, stories began appearing in the *Sun Journal* newspaper alleging that the city and state were about to ink a deal for a Wal-Mart distribution center, rumored to employ as many as 600 people. That turned out to be an exaggeration, but a secret deal *was* in the offing.

Throughout the fall, Wal-Mart officials wouldn't confirm they were seeking a financial deal in Lewiston, and city officials went along with this silence of the lambs. Just before Christmas, Lewiston Mayor Kaileigh Tara told the *Journal*, "About one month or so ago, I had to sign my life away to protect the confidentiality of the company." In so doing, city officials also signed away millions of dollars in public tax revenues for a company that had now reached a level of $217 billion in gross sales, surpassing Exxon Mobil to sit on top of the corporate world.

But Mayor Tara agreed to "sign her life away" to give Wal-Mart a very expensive and unfair incentive over its competitors. She was not alone. Complicit in the deal — for which the public had only two days advance notice — was Maine Governor Angus King, who told the press that the financial breaks given to Wal-Mart "levels the playing field." The Governor said dispensing such corporate welfare in the form of tax rebates, free land and road improvements, were necessary to give Maine — a "high tax state" — a shot at projects like a Wal-Mart food distribution center. Here's what it cost Lewiston to level the playing field:

- 61 acres of land — assessed at $300,600 — given to Wal-Mart, no charge
- relocation and expansion of sewer lines, $1 million
- a new sand and gravel pit for $940,000
- a new shed for sand and gravel, $800,000
- a commercial subdivision plan, $45,000
- water and sewer fee reimbursements, $18,300
- property tax reimbursements, $5.8 million

The total came to nearly $9 million from the city. The tax incremental financing deal came to 25 pages, plus a 65-page memo of agreement. Add to that another $8.4 million in candy from the state:

- A "Business Equipment Tax Reimbursement" program that will reimburse Wal-Mart over 12 years as much as $7.8 million on all personal property taxes
- $1.5 million for road relocations
- $180,000 in training money
- $348,750 in rebated state income tax that comes from its workers' payroll withholding

In return for this public largesse, Wal-Mart had to promise to employ 350 people, employ them for 30 hours per week, and pay them $12 an hour. That amounts to a salary of less than $19,000 a year before taxes.

Governor King may not have known or cared that Wal-Mart has built much of its distribution network on "incentives" that have cost local and state taxpayers millions of dollars in lost revenues. The *Sun Journal* researched six other Wal-Mart distribution centers, and found that Wal-Mart received nearly $75 million in incentives over the life of agreements with communities like Johnstown, New York. Taxpayers gave Wal-Mart nearly $9 million in Bradford, Pennsylvania; $6 million in Bedford, Pennsylvania; $10.4 million in Grove City, Ohio; nearly $11 million in Isle Creek, Ohio; and $13.7 million in Washington Courthouse, Ohio. According to the newspaper, the $16.7 million incentive package in Lewiston was one of the largest giveaways yet — totaling $47,852 per job in incentives. Incentives included sewer improvements, training grants, tax credits, and highway funds.

When the agreement was finally announced in Lewiston, Wal-Mart's real estate agent described the clandestine negotiating as "a wonderful process, a textbook example of the process" for locating a Wal-Mart facility. Only no one in the public got to read the book until it was published.

If this is a developer's "textbook case," then the plot boils down simply to welfare for the rich. This special deal will actually hurt competition in the state, and narrow consumer choice as other markets fail.

But was this King's Ransom really needed to attract Wal-Mart? Wouldn't they have come anyway? In Raymond, New Hampshire, residents got a Wal-Mart distribution center in 1996 more than twice the size of Lewiston's — and they didn't have to shell out sweets to get it. "We didn't offer them anything," admitted Raymond's town manager. "They offered *us* incentives. They bought the town a ladder truck for the fire department."

In comparison, Lewiston "signed its life away" for Wal-Mart. One of Wal-Mart's real estate vice presidents told local officials: "You will never have to duck around the corner" to avoid critics of this deal. The only vocal critic of the plan was Rex Rhoades, Executive Editor of the *Sun Journal* who framed his paper's position in black and white:

> It strikes me as grossly unfair that one of the poorest states in the union with the highest citizen tax burden must pay top dollar to attract low to middle income retail industry jobs...And it's not as if this is an export industry or these are research and development jobs. When Wal-Mart sells groceries, somebody else doesn't. We only

eat so much, making it a finite market. Competition is good, but it simply means that a grocery store job at Wal-Mart is subtracted from a grocery store job elsewhere.

One Lewiston city councilor who eventually voted for the plan nevertheless expressed his distaste for how Wal-Mart kept the "wonderful process" a wonderful secret. "I think it's despicable that this company chose to avoid public disclosure. People can say that's not the way it works. Well, not in my world."

But that's precisely how it works in Wal-Mart's world. Not only has Wal-Mart developed impressive first-hand corporate welfare experience, the company has used its overstated reputation as a tax-builder to get local officials to become accomplices to a plan that washes away its local business class.

In July 2002, a report from a non-profit research group, Policy Matters Ohio, claimed that Ohio taxpayers over the past year had offered Wal-Mart financial assistance totaling $10 million to build two food distribution centers and an eyeglass manufacturing plant. The study, *Wal-Mart Special: Ohio Tax Credits to America's Richest Retailer,* described how this corporate welfare came as part of an overly broad process from the Ohio Tax Credit Authority.

In the town of Washington Court House, in Fayette County, Ohio, Wal-Mart was given a job creation tax credit for 10 years estimated to be worth $2.6 million in the first year alone. To help the world's largest retailer dominate its smaller rivals with an 880,000-square-foot food distribution center, state taxpayers also tossed in $500,000 in roadwork, $200,000 in a training program, and $400,000 in community development block grant funds.

In the town of Columbus, in Franklin County, Ohio, Wal-Mart leased a 120,000-square-foot building to manufacture and distribute eyeglasses. The job creation tax credit there is worth about $2.2 million for Wal-Mart.

In a third location, Island Creek township, in Jefferson County, Ohio, taxpayers gave Wal-Mart a $2.8 million tax break on their food distribution center, plus $600,000 in road work, $483,600 in infrastructure grants, and a $650,000 warehouse equipment sales tax exemption.

The Policy Matters Ohio study suggested these projects did not meet the requirement under state law that "receiving the tax credit is a major factor in the [developer's] decision to go forward with the project." The report also indicated that this candy store of corporate welfare was not necessary to get Wal-Mart to locate in Ohio. In fact, at the Jefferson County distribution center, "the company announced its intent and started building the distribution center months before its job creation tax credit was approved." Ohio appeared to have violated its own guidelines for these tax breaks: "The project must not have already started at the Ohio site, or have been publicly announced to be undertaken at the site prior to approval by the Authority."

In the Washington Court House case, the report noted, "The Tax Credit Authority appears to have stepped around the intent of the law in determining the credit was a major factor in Wal-Mart's decision to invest in Ohio." In fact, the store was "already half built" before the agreement on a tax credit was signed.

The Policy Matters Ohio report concluded, "The process of awarding tax credits needs to be tightened." The group recommended that the Ohio Tax Credit Authority "should enforce its guideline not to award incentives when projects already have been publicly announced or begun. It also should consider very carefully whether to award incentives to distribution centers, many of which need to be located in a large state like Ohio."

The study found that Wal-Mart's statements about why the tax credit was important to their decision to locate in Ohio was not a public record, and that such explanations should be part of the public record for any citizen to obtain. Not only did Ohio taxpayers contribute to Wal-Mart's bottom line at the state level, but at the local level as well. In Jefferson County, Wal-Mart got an "enterprise zone" agreement which gave the company a 100% exemption on personal property tax on machinery, inventory and equipment for 10 years, and a 60% tax exemption on improvements to their building for 10 years. These give-aways were worth $3.6 million in savings to Wal-Mart — savings the company can use to gain a competitive advantage over local businesses not big enough to qualify for this welfare. In Washington Court House, the city financed more than $1.1 million of public infrastructure, and gave Wal-Mart a deal on land costs. Smaller firms help subsidize their larger rivals by contributing taxes to the state and local authority. The smaller companies are forced to subsidize the very companies that are putting them under.

Sometimes the offer of lavish public subsidies can create a backlash against Wal-Mart. I sat in a small insurance office in the town of Killingly, Connecticut on a Saturday in the late fall of 2002. The room was cold, waiting for the heat to kick in. With me were three residents. One of them was a town official. They had asked me to come down to talk about a proposed Wal-Mart distribution center on 350 acres of land. They were dead set against the plan, which they said would change their town forever.

Killingly is a small town (pop. 16,000) in the Northeast corner of the state. The economy never recovered from the 1950s, when six large curtain factories pulled down the shades and left. Wal-Mart was looking at a site for a 1.2 million square foot distribution center off Interstate 395, which cuts right through the center of town. The property Wal-Mart wanted needed a zoning change from "business park" to "industrial."

I had driven by the property earlier in the day. It was a beautiful natural forest. The surrounding area was predominately residential, mostly small, single-family homes along the roadside. The Wal-Mart facility would bring in nearly 700 trucks a day coming and going. This would cripple the on/off ramps from I-395 as well as the residential streets that access I-395.

There had been no official announcement that it was, in fact, Wal-Mart that was planning the facility — just that there was a "large corporation" interested. That's why the developer had requested a zone change. No one had been contacted to this point. The local town government and the Town Manager had tried to keep it hush-hush. The Town Manager, Town Council and the developer had all signed a confidentiality agreement with Wal-Mart stating that the project would be kept quiet until Wal-Mart gave the green light. The project was actually being referred to in Town Hall as "Project X."

The local real estate broker handling the deal had sent a letter to all the abutters, promising that the distribution center would bring the town $1 million a year in taxes, along with 1,000 new jobs paying an average of "close to $17 an hour." Data from another Wal-Mart warehouse showed not even an experienced mechanic makes more than $14 an hour. Without citing any evidence, the broker claimed the project would have "virtually no" impact on surrounding property values.

The local newspaper, the *Norwich Bulletin*, reported that the Killingly Economic Development Commission narrowly voted in favor of the zone change, 3-2, but the Conservation Commission unanimously voted to recommend against the zone change. The Conservation Commission was concerned about storm water runoff and environmental effects like noise pollution, intersection tie-ups and increased truck traffic. However, the Planning and Zoning Commission is the board that casts the binding vote.

When asked to verify that Wal-Mart was a potential developer for the parcel, Town Council Chairman Christian Sarantopoulos said he could not comment on the matter, noting the only item before the town was a zone change. "I don't believe it would be proper for me to comment on this," he told a *Bulletin* reporter. It was reported that Wal-Mart wanted $4.8 million in tax breaks (in the form of a "fixed mil rate" on their property for 20 years) to build their warehouse. The state was reportedly ready to kick in another $45 million in state aid, the newspaper noted.

The town official turned to me at the end of our strategy session. "If Wal-Mart can't build distribution centers without getting state and local tax breaks," he says, "maybe they shouldn't be building distribution centers."

"I can tell you this," he added, getting up from his chair to leave. "I won't support a single penny of local taxes to support them."

In turns out, he wasn't the only official in Killingly who felt that way. On March 24, 2003 only one member of the Killingly, Connecticut Planning and Zoning Commission voted in favor of a proposed Wal-Mart distribution center. In a stinging rebuke, Wal-Mart watched as its plan for a critical 1.12 million square foot distribution center went down for the count.

Wal-Mart officials told the *Hartford Courant* that they would have to search for another site for their oversized facility. The Wal-Mart distribution warehouse could not overcome the fact that the 350-acre parcel Wal-Mart wanted was not correctly zoned. The property was zoned for a business park, not an industrial park. The town's Planning and Zoning Commission said the town could find a higher use for the land than the low-paying jobs offered by Wal-Mart. The high price of public subsidies for a very rich corporation also left a bad taste for the project.

The chairman of the Town Council, who supported the Wal-Mart plan, dragged out the usual rhetoric about how Killingly would appear to be unfriendly to business because of this rejection. But the Council vice chair felt just the opposite. "I think that the original zone change to business park was a real ray of hope for Killingly, that we could attract some real professional jobs," vice chairman David Griffiths told the *Courant.* "I'm thrilled that the planning and zoning commission defeated the zone change."

Wal-Mart has been able to walk off with millions of dollars in tax breaks and other public subsidies over the years — all on the promise of jobs and taxes. Towns expect to see a payoff from this investment, but sometimes the pay-off never comes.

In May 2002, Wal-Mart announced that it was laying off 250 workers at its distribution center in Laurens, South Carolina. The layoffs took place in April. Yet the company announced it was continuing to move forward with another distribution center about 90 miles away in Shelby.

Cleveland County, South Carolina gave Wal-Mart roughly $175,000 over the next five years to build their center in Shelby. The city of Shelby and the county purchased 58 acres to donate to Wal-Mart. They also agreed to extend water, sewer and natural gas lines to the business. The cost of the land purchase was estimated at $240,000 and extending utility lines cost the Cleveland County Board of Commissioners $257,500.

Wal-Mart, which rarely talks about downsizing its workforce, said the Laurens center would be converted to just handling clothing, and they would try to find a place for the workers losing their jobs. "We like to keep our associates and we offer them opportunities to remain Wal-Mart associates because they're trained. We've offered opportunities to transfer to other distribution centers and we offer relocation assistance," said company spokesman Tom Williams.

The towns of Laurens and Cleveland County were played off against each other. One lost jobs, one gained them. Public money helped lure jobs from one town to the other, with very little net gain. It's a bargain Wal-Mart has been able to count on across the country — much to the dismay of its smaller competitors who have helped pay for the deal.

# Count 9
# Charity: False Advertising

*"Maybe the most important way in which we at Wal-Mart believe*
*in giving something back is through our commitment to using the power*
*of this enormous enterprise as a force for change."*

— Sam Walton, as quoted by Wal-Mart Foundation

A lot of money is spent to make you like Wal-Mart. In 2002, Wal-Mart spent nearly $1.85 million on advertising every day of the year. Most of this advertising money was for television and print ads. Most of that nearly $13 million a week on advertising was spent on image-making, and most of that image-making was designed to portray Wal-Mart as a family-friendly, good neighbor corporation. Wal-Mart likes to remind us that 10,000 executives, directors and securities analysts voted the retailer *Fortune* magazine's "Most Admired Company." But popularity within a clique on Wall Street is not always congruous with popularity with average Americans on Main Street. To portray the company as more than just a source of cheap underwear, Wal-Mart has spent a fortune crafting an image of philanthropy and good works. These stories are often told through vignettes, human-face tales of people whose lives were touched in some small way by the giant corporation. But the unadmirable things that go on inside a Wal-Mart store are not often seen or discussed.

What happened to Theresa Delzatto was not made into a thirty-second TV spot. Several days before the 1999 Christmas holiday, Delzatto, a severely disabled woman who is paralyzed from the neck down, received a check for $570 from Wal-Mart Stores, Inc. If this is all you knew of the story, you might think it was just another of those sweet stories you see on Wal-Mart TV commercials. There is a darker history behind this particular Wal-Mart check.

According to the *Hartford Courant*, on December 3, 1999, Theresa

Delzatto boarded a van with a chair lift for her motorized wheelchair, and went to Wal-Mart to do her Christmas shopping. Once in the store, the Wal-Mart Courtesy Desk assigned an 18-year-old Wal-Mart associate to help Delzatto shop. The Wal-Mart Associate helped Delzatto shop — and then helped herself.

The Wal-Mart employee used Delzatto's debit card to make her in-store purchases — but she never returned the card. Instead, with the help of her 17-year-old cousin who also worked at Wal-Mart, the two teenagers "went on a spending spree" with Delzatto's debit card, racking up more than $430 on Delzatto's bank account.

Delzatto only has a monthly income of $500, which comes from her Social Security disability check. She did not learn of the card's theft until several of her checks — including her rent check — bounced. Delzatto found herself running out of money for food. Delzatto turned to Margaret Drumgoole, a victim advocate for the Salvation Army, to help her get her money back.

On December 16th, Drumgoole contacted Wal-Mart, but the retailer was slow to respond. Delzatto was living check-to-check, and Wal-Mart's delay was disrupting her daily life. Drumgoole turned to the media to draw attention to what had happened to Delzatto. Only after Drumgoole released reports of the incident to the media did Wal-Mart respond. With public pressure mounting, and Christmas just three days away, Wal-Mart decided to cut a check for Delzatto — six days after Drumgoole brought the pathetic story of their employees' actions to Wal-Mart. The Wal-Mart check was enough to cover the lost money, and the bank fees for the checks that bounced. Nothing more.

At Wal-Mart headquarters in Bentonville, Arkansas, an apology was given to Delzatto through the media. "We apologize if there was any delay in responding to her," one Wal-Mart spokesman told the *Courant*. "We really want to help this person and make it right."

The police had arrest warrants out on the two Wal-Mart employees who financially wiped out this disabled 35-year-old woman. In addition, more than 30 people called to offer to donate money to help Delzatto. Delzatto said that any money she received above what she lost, she would donate to the Salvation Army's victim assistance program — the only program that had come through for her.

When you think of Wal-Mart's philanthropy, it is not Delzatto's name that comes to mind. Most of Wal-Mart's press releases tout its generous program of giving. In 1999, Wal-Mart claimed it contributed

$163 million to charity. The company had net sales of $167 billion—which calculates out to one-tenth of 1% of net sales, or the equivalent of a family with a $40,000 income giving $40 a year total to charity.

But that's not all. Much of Wal-Mart giving is not by the company — but by its customers or employees. In 2001, Wal-Mart boasted that "over $190 million was raised and contributed by our Associates and Customers and given back to our local communities." A considerable amount of giving from private individuals is packaged and presented in Wal-Mart's name.

At the local level, merchants will tell you that when the Girl Scouts and the Little League need support, it's the locally-owned companies who pitch in the lion's share of the support. The national chains have a few, symbolic causes to support, but the local merchant rarely says no to a community group.

Behind the plethora of "good works" stories at Wal-Mart — which local officials often quote — there are other stories that leave a bad taste. One associate who apparently got his contribution wires crossed is Brad Barritt, manager of the Wal-Mart store in Sterling, Colorado. His actions make a heart-warming Christmas story that might be titled: "The Wal-Mart Grinch."

According to Channel 7, an ABC affiliate in Colorado, local residents in Sterling were promoting a "Toys for Tots" (TFT) program in town, and had a drop-off box in the Wal-Mart. One TFT organizer, when she was told the box was nearly full, went to gather the toys. When she arrived at the store, there was a donation box — but no toys.

"I was devastated when I found it empty," she said. What Grinch would steal the toys from needy kids? It turns out the Grinch was none other than Wal-Mart manager Brad Barritt. The manager claimed he told TFT organizers that toys placed in the box needed to be wrapped in Wal-Mart bags to ensure that customers had bought the items before putting them in the box. (Otherwise the donations would have been directly from Wal-Mart.) Barritt removed the toys out of the Toys for Tots box — and put them back on the shelves for resale. Wal-Mart got the profit twice, and Toys for Tots got nothing. When the story came to light, Wal-Mart admitted that there must have been a mix-up, and that the company had already given $1,000 to TFT. "Not that that had anything to do with this situation," Barritt told ABC. "Only to say that as a corporation we are very community-minded. I'd hate to see a discrepancy over a few toys change that perception in the eyes of the public." After checking with corporate headquarters in Bentonville, Wal-Mart officials delivered

$425 worth of toys to the TFT local organizers.

For every tale of Wal-Mart generosity, there is also a darker tale. In 2003, Wal-Mart launched a new program called the "Associate in Critical Need Trust." Supported with Wal-Mart funds, the trust receives contributions from "members of management" to help employees of the company "during times of financial hardship due to death, catastrophic illness, or unforeseen circumstances. Wal-Mart is a caring employer that never forgets the Associates who make the company work." The Critical Need Trust, which was highlighted in Wal-Mart's 2003 Annual Report to stockholders, raised almost $3 million, and helped more than 2,800 families. The family of Joey Arena was not one of them.

Frank and Amy Arena, of Shawnee, Kansas, the parents of two year old Joey Arena, learned the literal meaning of the term "poster child." As reported in *New Times*, Frank and Amy Arena were told by doctors that Joey's heart murmur condition would require surgery costing as much as half a million dollars. Unless his heart defect was corrected, Joey would not live to see his fourth birthday.

Frank took a job at the Shawnee, Kansas Wal-Mart about seven months after Joey was born. Word soon filtered out among employees that Joey needed medical care beyond the family's meager budget. "We decided we wanted to raise some money for Joey," one employee told *New Times*. They selected the end of June 2002 to hold a "Joey Arena Dance to Health Day." About five weeks after Joey's operation, the employees at Wal-Mart, along with a local radio station and other sponsors, held the "life party" in the Wal-Mart parking lot to raise money for Joey's family — or so it seemed.

The Wal-Mart workers reached out to one of the company's favorite charities, the Children's Miracle Network, which became a co-sponsor of the event. Other vendors, like Coca-Cola signed on as sponsors. More than 30 businesses agreed to be official sponsors. Frank Arena started to grow concerned about the direction in which the event was heading. "About a week out was when I was starting to lose it," Arena admitted. "They were trying to attach Joey to Wal-Mart, and that's not what I wanted."

The event itself was considered a huge success for the local Wal-Mart in Shawnee. It was a blistering summer day, but thousands of people stopped by the Wal-Mart supercenter to dance, look at antique cars, or buy a $10 T-shirt with Joey's picture on it. Estimates were the event raised as much as $60,000. All of it was raised in Joey Arena's name — but none of it ever made it to Joey.

When the Arena family got a chance to meet directly with representatives from the Children's Miracle Network, Frank and Amy were informed that none of the money raised would actually go to Joey, or to pay for Joey's hospital bills. The Arenas claim that CMN told them that Joey was "the avenue to the money," in other words, the poster child for the cause. A representative of the CMN chapter in Kansas City explained that "apparently there was a misunderstanding...our organization does not do fund-raising for direct patient care." CMN gave money to hospitals in Kansas City, but not to Joey Arena. One small business owner who gave $350 to the event admitted: "It looks like the money is going to this little boy, and this little boy didn't get a dime. I'm very upset."

Wal-Mart's manager claimed that Frank and Amy knew what was going on, that the fund-raiser was "done in Joey's name and his honor." But the Wal-Mart worker who started the fund-raiser complained, "There's not a single employee in that store who understood that."

Several weeks after the event, Frank Arena and Wal-Mart parted company. Arena told reporters that he was terminated. Wal-Mart denies it. He is now working as a night security guard. He and Amy are paying off Joey's medical bills $10 a month.

In August 2003, the *Associated Press* reported that Frank and Amy Arena have filed a lawsuit against Wal-Mart in the U.S. District Court in Kansas City, seeking $75,000 in damages. In the lawsuit, the Arenas claim that the Wal-Mart fundraiser was billed as the "First Annual Joey Arena Dance for Health Day" and "A Special Event for a Special Little Boy." The Arena's lawyer told reporters that the family revealed their son's medical information because they expected to receive financial donations directly. The Arenas also say that volunteers told donors that their contribution was going to help pay for Joey Arena's medical expenses. The lawsuit says Joey's surgery ended up costing around half a million dollars.

Wal-Mart says that Frank Arena was given a check for $1,000 from the Wal-Mart Associate in Critical Need Trust. The company says it audited the fundraiser to see if the company made money after covering their costs, which including printing up T-shirts. The Arena family, and some Wal-Mart workers, expected that the publicity and good will which Wal-Mart received for this event would somehow benefit the child in whose name the event was held. Instead, the feel-good event ended up spreading enough bad feelings to fill up a parking lot.

Although charitable giving has become one of the pillars of corporate image at Wal-Mart, Sam Walton was never comfortable having his company measured by the extent of its corporate giving. In his autobiography, Walton said:

> We feel very strongly that Wal-Mart really is not, and should not be, in the charity business. We don't believe in taking a lot of money out of Wal-Mart's cash registers and giving it to charity for the simple reason that any debit has to be passed along to somebody — either our shareholders or our customers. . . By not designating a large amount of corporate funds to some charity which the officers of Wal-Mart may happen to like, we feel we give our shareholders more discretion in supporting their own charities.

Yet Wal-Mart is extremely self-conscious about its public image as a good corporate citizen. "Good. Works" and "Giving, Helping, Doing" are prominently featured in their reports to investors and customers. In late October 2003, Wal-Mart put out a press release announcing that the company had been named "the largest corporate cash giver" by *Forbes* magazine. In its press release, Wal-Mart claimed that it "contributed more than $150 million to support communities and local non-profit organizations." The company noted that its customers raised another $75 million, suggesting that at least one-third of Wal-Mart giving does not come from the company at all.

In the mid-1990s, Wal-Mart began featuring pictures of crippled children in its Annual Reports. "Even Wal-Mart's reputation as the largest corporate donor to the Children's Miracle Network Telethon," the company said, "is the result of thousands of Associates collecting dimes and dollars throughout the country in locally based efforts to help children with life-threatening diseases." Those "dimes and dollars" came from citizens — not from the company.

Over the years, Wal-Mart has aggressively advertised its "Good.Works" campaign, from the Students in Free Enterprise program, to the National World War II Memorial campaign. Every contribution appears to be a photo opportunity. In 1996, Wal-Mart ran a picture of a Children's Miracle Network poster child in its Annual Report. In 1997 the company's Annual Report displayed a crippled child from Lewiston, Pennsylvania wearing "an honorary Associate's name tag and giving smiles and greetings to everyone she passes." The following year, the company told the story of "Baby Grace," a premature baby born in Florence, South Carolina. In 1999 Wal-Mart pictured 3-year-old Luke Harbur of Overland Park, Kansas, who suffered from Alagille Syndrome, a rare disease that can lead to liver failure. Luke was pictured standing next to a chart showing Wal-Mart employees as "the largest charitable fund-raising force in the United States."

In 2000 Wal-Mart highlighted that the company "was ranked as the number one good corporate citizen by the 1999 Cone/Roper Report." In 2002, Wal-Mart printed a sidebar in its Annual Report that the company had been ranked number 17 on "America's most visible companies with the best reputation," according to the Reputation Institute. Companies were ranked in six categories, from workplace environment to products and services. "The study placed Wal-Mart third in 'social responsibility' behind Johnson & Johnson and Coca-Cola, both of which are Wal-Mart vendors."

This type of public relations advertising is called "cause-related marketing." Consultants like Boston-based Cone/Roper say they teach corporations how to "impact social issues and the bottom line" at the same time. They call it "Cause Branding," a form of strategic philanthropy. Such goal-focused giving "helps companies integrate values and social issues into brand equity and organizational identity."

Carol Cone, one of the founders of the Cone/Roper, has written that the world's leading corporations, like Wal-Mart, "are turning a concern for causes into long-term brand equity." In other words, who a company gives money to can help shape its reputation, "brand personality" and "organizational identity." It's all about "enhanced brand equity and credibility." Stripping away the New Age language, aligning a company with a good cause is good for sales.

In 1993, Cone/Roper began producing consumer studies to show how consumers would respond to cause marketing. According to that early Cone/Roper study:

- 84% of consumers said they have a more positive image of a company if it is doing something to make the world better
- 66% said they would switch brands to support a cause they cared about
- 62% said they would switch retail stores to support a cause

In a 2000 survey of 12,000 consumers in 12 European countries, Corporate Social Responsibility Europe reported that, in a one year period, two in five consumers purchased a product because of its ties with a popular cause, or a product labeled as social, ethical or environmental. 20% of those polled even said they would pay more for such "ethical" products. In a comprehensive study conducted in 2000 by U.K.-based Business in the Community, 88% of consumers admitted they were aware of cause marketing programs and 77% said that such programs have positively changed their behavior or perceptions.

Cone explained that shoppers will reward companies who promote popular causes. "Having a cause program has become a 'must do' in the marketplace for companies to remain competitive," Cone noted. Her company tells executives that a retailer's reputation as being a responsible business is the most important factor to consumers in deciding whether or not to buy a brand – after price and quality. A corporation's social responsibility is considered more important to the consumer than its advertising.

Cause-related marketing can help a national or international company to "better identify" with its local markets by linking themselves with community organizations — especially companies that have generated significant controversy at the local level. Nearly 9 out of 10 Executives in the Cone/Roper poll in 2000 said that "gaining community support" was a key outcome of strategic philanthropy.

In the 2002 Cone/Roper Report, the authors concluded that in the aftermath of Enron and WorldCom, "It is more important than ever for companies to be socially responsible." Wal-Mart, the company that was exploiting children for pennies a day in Asian sweatshops, was investing millions of dollars to fabricate a positive brand image by continually promoting its concern for disabled children all across America.

Just about the same time as the Enron scandal, the Domini Index dropped Wal-Mart from its family of funds. Domini is an investment firm specializing exclusively in socially responsible investing. The Domini Social Equity Fund is the oldest and largest socially and environmentally screened index fund in the world, according to the company. Domini manages more than $1.3 billion in assets for individual and institutional investors "who wish to integrate social and environmental criteria into their investment decisions". As far back as 1994, Domini used its investments to file Annual Stockholder's Resolutions at Wal-Mart annual meetings. In 1994, Domini filed a resolution about the company's equal opportunity employment record. At the time, Wal-Mart was one of the fund's largest holdings.

At the same time that the Wal-Mart Foundation was running stories about its concern for disabled children, Wal-Mart Stores was paying out a $6.8 million fine to settle 13 disability discrimination lawsuits brought by the federal Equal Employment Opportunities Commission. The lawsuits were filed as a result of Wal-Mart violations in 11 states of the Americans with Disabilities Act. Under the settlement, Wal-Mart agreed to remove all disability-related questions from its job applications.

Jeremy Fass and William Darnell, two deaf men, were filing a lawsuit against Wal-Mart for discrimination against the disabled. It took several years and a lawsuit by the federal government to get Wal-Mart to hire them. Fass and Darnell filed complaints with the federal Equal Employment Opportunity Commission when they were both rejected for jobs on the night shift at a Wal-Mart in Tucson, Arizona. Neither Fass nor Darnell ever got an interview callback even though Fass' mother, who worked at the store, knew they were hiring. When they inquired further, they were informed there were no jobs.

The EEOC was joined by the Arizona Disability Law Center in a federal lawsuit in the spring of 1997. Two and a half years later, Wal-Mart admitted they wronged these two men. "We realize that in this instance, we did something wrong at the local level," a spokesman for the company told the *Associated Press*. The settlement Wal-Mart agreed to required the company to offer Fass and Darnell jobs, retroactive to September of 1995. Wal-Mart hired Fass and Darnell at $8 an hour. The company also paid $57,500 in attorneys' fees and costs to the prosecuting agencies. Wal-Mart also hired a sign-language interpreter during a two-week training period for Fass and Darnell, as required. But Wal-Mart made no admission of discriminatory behavior. Wal-Mart also agreed to make changes in its training programs to accommodate deaf employees.

A year and a half later, the EEOC asked a federal judge in Tucson, Arizona to find Wal-Mart in contempt of court in the Fass and Darnell settlement. The EEOC brought Wal-Mart back to court charging that the company failed to fulfill the settlement agreement. Specifically, Wal-Mart never developed training materials for hearing-impaired employees, and had not provided its managers with disabilities training. In addition, the EEOC claimed that Wal-Mart refused to allow federal officials inside Wal-Mart stores to verify compliance with the settlement. "Because Wal-Mart has steadfastly refused to satisfy its court-ordered obligations, we remain extremely concerned for hearing-impaired individuals in Arizona and throughout the country who seek employment with Wal-Mart or are currently employed," the Phoenix EEOC said.

Wal-Mart said it was surprised by the charges, because it had complied with virtually all of the terms of the settlement. A federal judge later ordered Wal-Mart to make a television commercial admitting it violated the Americans with Disabilities Act. U.S. District Judge William Browning fined Wal-Mart $750,200 after finding it in contempt for not complying with the consent decree.

A Wal-Mart spokesman told the *Los Angeles Times* that the company never admitted discrimination in settling the suit. "Even if we are judged to have violated the consent decree, there were provisions of the decree that went beyond the ADA itself," Wal-Mart was quoted as saying. "So we're uncertain how the judge determined the ADA was violated." The company was ordered to make a 30-second commercial and air it for two weeks on major Arizona stations. "This was not something that had been discussed with us previously," Wal-Mart complained.

In retailing, image is paramount. At great expense to the company, Wal-Mart has cultivated a brand image of a caring, giving, positive force for community betterment. Wal-Mart has invested more money than perhaps any other retailer to sustain this perception of the good citizen. The profitability of the company is directly connected to this corporate image. Reporters have often told me that Wal-Mart will not grant interviews on subjects that might tarnish the corporate image. To protect corporate image is a time-consuming, challenging endeavor. The cracks in this image are found at the day-to-day operational level of the company: how it treats its workers, its communities, its vendors, and most importantly, its customers.

# Count 10:
# Danger to Public Safety

*"A forklift, operated by an uncertified driver was working the next aisle...he pushed
a pallet containing five-gallon plastic buckets of laundry detergent weighing 38 pounds
each and boxes of large containers of fabric softener over onto Mom.
She lived for about thirty minutes, in horrible pain,
conscious, and aware of her approaching death."*

— Judith Cain Dotson describing her mother's death in a Sam's Club in Tulsa, Oklahoma,
from a letter dated February 2001

At Wal-Mart, the number one business principle is "the customer is always right." Sam Walton wrote in *The Boss' Creed,* "The greatest measure of our success is how well we please the customer." Yet the company has been willing to risk this success by putting its customers in harm's way.

Prices are not the only thing falling at Wal-Mart. The merchandise drops as well. There have been injuries and deaths to customers from falling merchandise. People have literally died to shop at Wal-Mart. In its employee handbook, Wal-Mart says it is "committed to maintaining a safe shopping environment for our customers and members." The company says it wants to "help our customers enjoy a pleasant, safe shopping experience and control a major source of expense to our Company."

When 29-year-old Sherry Haley went to her local Wal-Mart in Farmington, Maine on February 3, 1998, instead of walking out with merchandise, she left with a lawsuit. As a result of her injury, the mother of three says she is now "basically unemployable." Haley sued Wal-Mart for negligence in U.S. District Court after her shoulder was injured when a stack of car mechanic devices known as "creepers" fell on her.

111

Creepers are wooden skids on wheels that allow a mechanic to slide easily under cars to make repairs.

A safety expert testified that Wal-Mart had stacked the creepers in an unsafe manner, according to the *Associated Press*. Wal-Mart denied the devices — which weigh 8 pounds each — were dangerously stacked. But a federal magistrate judge disagreed, ordering Wal-Mart to pay Haley $22,167 in medical damages, and $50,000 for pain, suffering and permanent impairment. Haley needed shoulder surgery after her injury. Her surgeon estimated that she has 25% impairment in her upper body, and 15% impairment in her whole body since the injury. Denying culpability, a Wal-Mart spokesman told the *Associated Press*, "We don't believe there was anything wrong in the way the creepers were displayed at our store. At this time, we are exploring our options."

The *Los Angeles Times* published an article about fatal injuries caused by falling merchandise at Wal-Mart. The victims included Dolly Cain, a 70-year-old woman who was killed at a Sam's Club in Briscoe, Oklahoma in 1985. Another child was killed by a falling wardrobe at Sam's Club in Abilene, Texas in 1996. A Wal-Mart cabinet fell on a 2-year-old girl at a Virginia Beach, Virginia store in 1997, fatally injuring her. Wal-Mart claims its workers are properly trained, and conduct "bump tests" to see if merchandise is properly stacked — but it is often the workers who "bump" a rack over onto a customer.

Over a six-year period, Wal-Mart recorded 26,000 customer injuries from falling merchandise, and another 7,000 employees injured. "When you consider that we have 100 million customers a week, the number of falling merchandise cases is very small," explained Les Copeland, a Wal-Mart spokesman. "Our overall track record is very good." According to a January 2001 article in *The Boston Globe*, personal injury claims against Wal-Mart from falling merchandise number roughly 4,300 a year. Tom Williams, a Wal-Mart spokesman, told *The Globe* that in 1998 Wal-Mart had "no more than 2,500 physical injuries of any significance, including customers who dropped boxes on their feet."

During a falling merchandise case, *Scharrel v. Wal-Mart Inc.*, the court ordered Wal-Mart to produce a list of all claims in which customers were injured by falling merchandise at their stores nationwide. The result was a 300-plus page report that revealed that from 1989 to 1994 there were 17,180 claims of falling merchandise injuries against the company. Gary M. Bakken, of Analytica Systems International, Inc., in Tucson, Arizona, analyzed the first 7,036 of those claims and concluded that 34% of the analyzed records involved an impact to the head. Of the remaining injuries, 26% involved the lower extremities, 10% involved multiple injuries, 7% percent involved the upper extremities and the remainder was divided up among back, shoulder, neck, and torso.

"When a jury returns with a multi-million verdict," says attorney Jeff Hyman, who has represented plaintiffs in many court trials against Wal-Mart, "the community is saying that Wal-Mart isn't doing things right. But they don't seem to have gotten the message." The high stacking of merchandise, called sky shelves, is an image stores create to suggest a cornucopia of products. It also allows a retailer to cut down on warehouse space by stacking their inventory over the customers' heads. Since customers cannot reach up the shelves, they present unique dangers to shoppers. One judge cited by *The Los Angeles Time*s said that shoppers should not bear responsibility for the store's lack of safety. "You'd have to wear safety helmets indoors," the judge said, "and I'm not prepared to do that."

Wearing hard hats at Wal-Mart may sound like a joke, but a falling object at any of their stores does not have to be heavy to inflict serious damage, because as a falling object gains momentum, it gains weight. A 10-pound object falling 10 feet can have a force of impact of 1,200 pounds, enough to fracture a cranial bone.

According to federal Occupational Safety and Hazards Administration (OSHA) rules, merchandise is supposed to be "stacked, blocked, interlocked and limited in height so that they are stable and secure against sliding or collapse." But OSHA maintains absolutely no records of serious injuries or deaths to shoppers — only to employees. In March 2002, *Professional Safety* magazine estimated that "consumer injuries in warehouse superstores across the country may be in the tens of thousands each year."

The first state to address the injuries and deaths at stores like Wal-Mart was California. In October 2001, legislation was signed into law in California that begins to address the safety concerns in stores like Wal-Mart. The California State Firefighters' Association offered the legislation. The bill, SB 486, requires an owner, manager, or operator of a working warehouse to secure merchandise stored on shelves higher than 10 feet above the sales floor by installing safety devices such as rails or fencing. It also requires them to prevent customers from entering aisles before removing the safety devices and moving merchandise. Since July 2002, California law requires all working warehouses to make their sky shelving safer. In addition, a working warehouse employing more than 50 employees is required to annually submit to the Division of Occupational Safety and Health a report of all serious injuries or deaths occurring to customers at the establishment during the preceding year. Under the law, the division is required to submit to the Senate Committee on Industrial Relations and to the Assembly Committee on Labor and Employment an annual statistical report summarizing those customer injuries and deaths, and recommending preventive legislation, if necessary.

In December 2000, I introduced legislation in the Massachusetts General Court that would have required retailers to report customer injuries and deaths to the state, and force companies to give consumers hard hats to wear in certain superstore areas. The bill was opposed by the Massachusetts retailing lobby, and died in committee. Today, Wal-Mart provides no accounting of public injuries or deaths to any state or federal authorities. Even though thousands of injuries take place every year, there is no public record of any such occurrences — except when the customer sues the company for damages.

As *Professional Safety* concluded, "Warehouse superstores invite the unknowing, untrained general public (including the elderly and small children) into what is in effect a 'working warehouse.' Millions of people shop in these stores each year — and none of them expect to be injured (or killed) while doing so. Yet, customer fatalities and large numbers of injuries occur each year...customers should not have to face an increased risk of injury simply to get variety and lower prices."

# Count 11:
# Abandonment of Premises

As quietly as Wal-Mart tries to slip into a town, sometimes they try to leave just as noiselessly.

In Seneca, South Carolina, the new Wal-Mart was located right across the street from an existing Wal-Mart. This is the same pattern Wal-Mart followed in Anderson, South Carolina, when it opened a supercenter in January 1999 and closed down its discount store. As of mid-September 2000, Wal-Mart already had 17 stores in South Carolina on the market to lease or sell, ranking South Carolina 8th highest in the nation for empty, "available" Wal-Mart stores. Wal-Mart told shoppers in Seneca that their current 93,000-square-foot store was "not a very big store to shop in" and that the new supercenter "would mean a little more room to shop in on Saturday." But it was really opened for the convenience of Wal-Mart stockholders, not to make Saturday a roomier shopping day. The true beneficiaries were Wal-Mart investors, because the superstore format is much more profitable than the smaller discount stores.

In Plymouth, Massachusetts, Wal-Mart landed with a lot more fanfare than the Pilgrims. The company opened up a discount store in 1995, which required the city to remove its historic first library stone by stone to another location. But eight short years later, Wal-Mart was seeking approval for a larger supercenter at another location in Plymouth, while preparing to abandon its 123,028-square-foot discount store.

"Quite frankly," said Tom Seay, Wal-Mart's former Executive Vice

President for Real Estate Construction, "I think the fact that we relocate stores — and we relocate a lot of them — is a well-known fact in the development community." Just how portable Wal-Mart is, however, is not well known by the shopping public. In their 1998 Annual Report, Wal-Mart featured a short profile of its Real Estate division, under the title: "The Wal-Mart nobody knows." According to the company, Wal-Mart is the "largest owner and manager of retail space in the country."

Like a reptile crawling out of its skin, Wal-Mart has shed hundreds of stores to move on to bigger facilities. Most of these relocations have been in towns where Wal-Mart shuts down a discount store to open up a larger supercenter a few miles, or even blocks, away. "As [Wal-Mart] rolls out new supercenter prototypes," the company explains, "it must also find uses for existing relocated stores after they are closed." But often these empty shells sit like huge concrete caverns lining the roadways.

Since 1988, when Wal-Mart shifted to the superstore prototype, it has been engaged in a no-gain game for the local economy in hundreds of American towns. Wal-Mart will open up a supercenter — a discount store combined with a grocery store — frequently at the cost of closing down its existing discount store, and always at the expense of local merchants. The supercenter pulls in a higher level of sales volume from the local trade area, but in addition, threatens the viability of existing grocery stores.

Presque Isle, Maine is a typical example of this zero sum game. In August 1999, Wal-Mart filed plans in City Hall to dramatically increase the size of its store to create a Wal-Mart superstore. A community of roughly 12,500 people, Presque Isle had a discount Wal-Mart since 1993, which measured in at 97,000 square feet. When Wal-Mart built their store, the city agreed to let them expand by another 30,000 square feet at a later date. Six years later, Wal-Mart came back with plans to double the size of the store to 185,000 square feet. The only difference between the existing Wal-Mart and the supercenter was the addition of groceries. But Presque Isle already had a 50,000-square-foot IGA, a 5,000-square-foot IGA, a 7,000-square-foot Sure Fine, and a 40,000-square-foot Graves Shop N Save. The Wal-Mart expansion would be right next door to the Shop N Save, which had been a fixture in the city since 1935.

Nearby the existing Wal-Mart in Presque Isle, is the struggling Aroostook Center Mall, which has lost a Rite Aid, a J.C. Penney and a Sears. Ames closed its doors six months after Wal-Mart first came to town. The City's Community Development Director called the doubling of Wal-Mart's size "a relatively simple set of changes." The *Star Herald* newspaper suggested that a Wal-Mart supercenter would boost employment from 200 to 400 jobs, but if the Shop N Save closes, that will eliminate 100 jobs from whatever jobs Wal-Mart creates. Others in town wondered how long the Kmart at Aroostook Center Mall would last. The theory in Presque Isle seemed to be the more grocery stores built, the hungrier the people would get. But none of this development was really expanding the retail pie, just slicing it thinner for the smaller players.

As a direct consequence of Wal-Mart's changing its major growth vehicle from a discount store to a supercenter, the company has left hundreds of its own stores empty. This has happened so many times across America, that the phenomenon has been given a name: the "Empty Box Syndrome." The *Bucks County [PA] Courier Times* editorialized on the subject in March 2001:

> When they started showing up several years ago, who knew that "big" stores someday would produce a big dilemma? That some of the businesses housed by these warehouse-sized structures would have surprisingly short life spans? And that the cavernous buildings left behind, some large enough to house small cities, would be of little interest to other retailers? Or that they would prove not easily convertible to other uses? Well, now we know...Eventually, local governments might have to take a loss to realize a gain. To make the land marketable, they might have to condemn and then tear down these architectural dinosaurs.

Wal-Mart is the industry leader in the empty box syndrome. By September 2000, there were 390 "available" Wal-Marts on the market, 47 of which had come on the market within the past six months. "Sometimes we outgrow our stores," Wal-Mart Realty admits. The company outgrew more than 25 million square feet of former stores. These facilities were located in 36 states. There were 14 states with 10 or more empty Wal-Marts, with 292 stores (75%) leased by Wal-Mart, and only 98 (25%) owned by the company. Even though some stores were sold or leased, another 40 to 50 stores were added to the available list every six months. The states leading the empty store count were:

Wal-Mart Empty Box Count, 2000

Texas: 50
Florida: 41
Georgia: 35
Tennessee: 25
Alabama: 20
Louisiana: 19
Arkansas: 18
South Carolina: 17
Mississippi: 17
Kentucky: 14
Oklahoma: 13
North Carolina: 13
Missouri: 13

More than 102 stores on the market were over 100,000 square feet, and many of them were built in the late 1980s or 1990s, and were hardly what you would call "spent stores." These dead or dying stores were due to one factor: when Wal-Mart shifted from the discount store boxes to supercenters, they began closing discount stores where they could not easily enlarge them into supercenters. Many of these stores were not "outgrown" but mothballed because the company decided they could pump more money through their "units" by adding a grocery store.

Wal-Mart said that their aisles were crowded and stores too small, but when you look at the size of some of the available buildings, it's clear that this trail of empty stores — a form of retail road kill — was left behind because Wal-Mart wanted larger sales figures, not larger aisles. At first just a southern phenomenon, the dead store count has been moving north and west as Wal-Mart moves its supercenter expansion into those areas. In Maine, for example, there were 3 stores on the available list by 2002, where there were none in February of 1999.

Wal-Mart listed a 114,000-square-foot store in Bangor, Maine on Springer Drive as an available building. The Bangor store had been listed for at least six months before the local community learned of a plan to build a new Wal-Mart in Bangor. Even as Wal-Mart was telling local people that discussions were in the "preliminary stages," the "old"

Wal-Mart store in Bangor had already been put up for sale. In May 2003, the state of Maine rejected the proposed Wal-Mart supercenter in Bangor. The "old" Bangor Wal-Mart was never emptied, because the supercenter project fell through. But local residents never knew their existing store was slated to close.

A similar incident occurred in Davenport, Iowa, where residents were startled to learn in February 2001 that Wal-Mart had already listed its current discount store as available — even before the company had received a rezoning of land to open up a new store.

Real estate companies have learned that Wal-Mart changes stores as casually as you and I change shoes. All this moving about has left many landowners with broken leases and nothing but a breach of contract lawsuit on their hands.

The *Philadelphia Inquirer* described the empty store situation in February 2001:

> The suburban landscape is littered with these rotting carcasses — big, boxy, wide-aisled reminders of stores that once teemed with wild-eyed bargain hunters. They went by names such as Hechinger, Caldor and Service Merchandise — expansive stores that ushered in an age of seemingly unlimited discount purchasing potential. But the jobs-hungry communities that ardently lured them, that believed the corporate mantra of the 1980s that 'economies of scale' made those companies indestructible, now find themselves faced with the graffiti-strewn mess left behind when the economy rolled right over them. The towns are saddled with the prospect of spending millions to demolish the buildings, letting them rot, or tackling the nearly impossible task of peddling them to someone else. And the salvation being dangled in front of these hard-pressed communities, once again, is ever more gigantic models.

Since 1988, Wal-Mart has been involved in the systematic closure of its discount stores. The company's major accomplishment of the 1990s was capturing other merchants' grocery market share. As the numbers below suggest, Wal-Mart increased its superstores by ten-fold during the second half of the 1990s, adding an average of 108 superstores per year. But at the same time, Wal-Mart closed almost 9%

of its discount stores, mostly in the south. The company's superstores increased by 1,190 units, while its discount stores dropped by 385. The total number of stores increased by 40%. The major change is that the superstore went from 3% of the store mix in 1994, to 44% by 2003, and the discount stores fell from 97% of the mix to 56%.

| Wal-Mart Store Type | 1994 | 2003 |
|---|---|---|
| Discount Stores | 1,953 | 1,568 |
| Superstores | 68 | 1,258 |
| Total | 2,021 | 2,826 |

The *Philadelphia Inquirer* listed a total of 93 empty big box stores in nine counties in New Jersey and Pennsylvania as of January 2001:

Big box glut has forced many aging stores to go belly-up. And after the merchandise is cleared off the racks, their buildings sit behind. The abandoned behemoths have become an eyesore on the landscape and a financial and security liability for local governments helpless to do much about them. "It's not easy to find substitute uses once these boxes are abandoned," said Patty Elkis, a senior planner at the Delaware Valley Regional Planning Commission. "They make the whole area look bad and people stay away."

The excess real estate dumped on the market by Wal-Mart often was of little interest to other merchants — not only because Wal-Mart would not allow them to be used by competing retailers — but also because the buildings themselves were not of great value. "They are crappy buildings," admits Donovan Rypkema, an economic development consultant. "There is no logic in reinvesting in them at all." One builder in Massachusetts included in his portfolio that he had built Wal-Mart stores for the company for only $30 per square foot — a very low construction figure. Wal-Mart manages to put a happy smile even on these empty buildings. Company spokesman John Bisio calls these vacancies, "The sign of a healthy economy."

Wal-Mart has proven itself to be the preeminent portable company — its assets are like a moveable feast. Although the company says very few of its stores have failed, some are unprofitable, and hundreds of others are simply shut down to make way for supercenters with wider aisles. This makes Wal-Mart the largest producer of empty retail stores in America — and the world. At Wal-Mart's 2003 annual meeting in Fayetteville, Arkansas, the company's Chief Financial Officer, Tom Schoewe, told stockholders, "There are a lot of discount stores we can convert to supercenters. It's an incredible growth opportunity."

But holding all these dead assets actually has created a fiscal drag on the company. In August 2003, Wal-Mart reported in a USA Today story that it had sold $13 million worth of dead stores to other companies over the past year. But because newly abandoned stores appear every month, the Wal-Mart inventory of empty stores remains unsurpassed by any other retailer currently in business. In the summer of 2003 when I told a reporter that Wal-Mart had nearly 400 dead stores on the market, a company spokesman said I was wrong. The figure was closer to 300, the company said.

There is another dark side to this "dark store" trend. In the real estate world a number of companies that supply land to Wal-Mart, expected a long and profitable landlord-tenant relationship. They have found themselves in front of a judge instead.

The U.S. Circuit Courts of Appeals have seen repeated cases of landlords in Tennessee, Alabama, Louisiana, Oklahoma, and South Carolina who have leased property to Wal-Mart, only later to sue for breach of contract when Wal-Mart moved out and left its stores empty.

When a real estate company in Jefferson County, Texas brought a breach of contract lawsuit against Wal-Mart in the early 1990s, it cited five other lawsuits in which "Wal-Mart interfered with contractual relationships."

In Lebanon, Tennessee, a real estate company sued Wal-Mart for $54 million, accusing the retailer of moving out of its lease 11 years early, despite the fact that the landlord spent $1 million to increase the store's size. Wal-Mart offered to fill the empty space with a Bud's Discount Center (which has since ceased all operations), but the landlord relied on a lease agreement with Wal-Mart to get a percentage of gross sales each year in addition to rent. The Bud's store would not come close to the estimated $28 million in sales that the Wal-Mart was doing. Wal-Mart had moved out of this site to build a new supercenter several miles away. "There's a lot of tenants in that shopping center depending on Wal-Mart being there whose business will be adversely affected," said the lawyer for the landlord.

In Catoosa, Oklahoma, a U.S. Bankruptcy Court found that Wal-Mart had breached its lease with Oklahoma Plaza Investors. Wal-Mart left its store with 8 years still to go on a 20-year lease. Wal-Mart removed its inventory and fixtures, locked the doors, and covered the windows with brown paper. The Court ruled, "This is a desertion of the premises and a breach of the lease . . . Wal-Mart should be required to keep its promises . . . [Wal-Mart] should not be allowed to break their promise to operate a discount store or to ignore an agreement that desertion of the premises would be a default." Wal-Mart argued that it was still using the premises by holding meetings there on occasion, and for storage. But the Court ruled, "The use of the premises for storage or meetings after a complete closing of the store is a mere subterfuge to try to avoid the consequences of an obvious desertion."

Many of the court cases are not so obvious, and often developers and landlords end up losing their rent on legal technicalities found in their open-ended lease agreements with Wal-Mart. These cases can also take a decade to work through the courts.

Landowners and communities should know by now not to expect a long-term relationship with Wal-Mart. Nowata, Oklahoma was described by *The New York Times* as "a city that Wal-Mart ditched." "When Wal-Mart pulls up and departs," the *Times* wrote in March 1995, "it leaves both a hole in the old downtown, and a gash across the entire local economy." Wal-Mart arrived with its suitcase already packed in Nowata, Pawhuska, and Bixby, Oklahoma. When it opened a supercenter in Bartlesville, the other three communities lost their Wal-Mart discount stores. Children playing in the schoolyards in Nowata were overheard by *The New York Times* reporter as chanting: "Wal-Mart, Fall-Apart."

# Count 12:
# Reckless Endangerment

*"Wal-Mart and/or its law firms have systematically engaged in a
conspiracy to fraudulently prevent the production of evidence...
relating to Wal-Mart's knowledge regarding crimes on their premises."*

--Attorney Alto V. Watson III, *Donna Meissner v. Wal-Mart Stores*, 1999

Mayor Morris Vance was in a tight spot.

On the one hand, his community of Vista, California, was faced with what the *San Diego Union-Tribune* called a "sharp spike" in crime in the early summer of 2003. On the other hand, his city was dealing with a severe revenue problem. The overall crime rate in Vista had skyrocketed by 24% over the past year. The Mayor blamed the weak economy and an unemployment rate — just shy of 5%. But one of the Mayor's law enforcement officials told reporters he had the real answer: Wal-Mart.

Sheriff's Lieutenant Grant Burnett told the *Union-Tribune* that the town's rising crime rate was due to a steady stream of shoplifters arrested at Wal-Mart. Every case had to be booked by local police, according to the newspaper. "Wal-Mart brought in its own loss prevention people," Burnett explained, "and that added tremendously to the amount of burglary arrests for shoplifters."

Every time the local cops are called in to arrest people for shoplifting at Wal-Mart, it takes police time and money to complete the incident report. One of the unspoken municipal costs of doing business with Wal-Mart is the growing city expense of processing Wal-Mart shoplifting cases. No doubt this expense was not part of the original Wal-Mart presentation when the company first pitched its store to Vista officials.

Municipal officials rarely consider, or mention, the significant added financial burden that servicing a Wal-Mart supercenter can bring to the city or town budget. Township officials in West Sadsbury, Pennsylvania certainly did not see this added cost coming. When the Wal-Mart store was built in their community, they were told municipal costs would be no big deal. "Early on," admits West Sadsbury Police Chief John Slauch, "the developers said [the shopping center] wouldn't have a great impact. That's not true." Unfortunately, what the police discovered was that Wal-Mart served as a magnet for shoppers—and criminals as well. When the town's police contract came up for renewal in September 2003, town officials went over the numbers to quantify the negative impact on law enforcement costs the Wal-Mart store had caused in their community. "I think we're up to our 200th arrest," Don Markwood, the town's police supervisor, told the *Parkesburg Post Ledger* newspaper. The newspaper reported the town's increasing concern over the rising costs associated with police services specifically tied to Wal-Mart's operations.

According to figures provided by Chief Slauch, in 2002 more than 10% of all police calls originated from the shopping center where Wal-Mart was an anchor. Of that percentage of calls, 34% came specifically from Wal-Mart. In the first five months of 2003, 14% of all police calls were from the shopping center, and of those calls, 40% were from Wal-Mart.

According to the West Sadsbury police, the arrest rate had tripled within the past year. The shopping center paid only $8,000 in property taxes to the town. The community received no reimbursement for police work directly from Wal-Mart or the developer. The Police Chief noted that other towns in Bucks County got money from the developer to cover security costs.

"When you have one entity getting the calls," the Police Chief noted, "the taxpayers are paying. We're handling a lot of complaints and spending time to investigate. The amount of time being spent far outweighs the revenue."

In a better world, the only illegal activity at a Wal-Mart supercenter would involve petty crimes like shoplifting. Unfortunately, the crime problem at Wal-Mart is much graver. One could argue that crime at Wal-Mart is not that different than crime at any other large retailer. In fact, most malls attract criminals. But Wal-Mart has come under growing criticism not so much for its crime statistics — but for the manner in which it responds to customers who are victimized by criminals.

According to the *Associated Press*, Wal-Mart was hit with a $2.16 million verdict in Florida in July 1998 for violating federal law that bans the sale of handgun bullets to anyone under 21. Sandra Coker, whose husband was murdered in a 1991 robbery at a Pensacola auto parts store, sued Wal-Mart over her husband's death. The murdered was committed by two teenagers using bullets illegally sold by Wal-Mart. The teens involved are now on death row in Florida. The Supreme Court in Florida found that Wal-Mart was negligent in illegally selling handgun ammunition to the teens, who proceeded to use the .32 caliber bullets in the auto parts store robbery and murder.

The Florida Appeals court that heard the case said that Congress passed the ammunition law on the assumption that selling bullets to minors would produce dangerous outcomes. Wal-Mart appealed the court's ruling to the Supreme Court, but lost.

It took Coker seven years of court wrangling to receive justice and compensation for her husband's death. Seven years of fighting in the courts to prevail over Wal-Mart. Instead of receiving any sympathy or financial help from Wal-Mart, the widow had to take aim at the world's biggest retailer through the courts.

Understandably, Wal-Mart does not like to reveal the extent of its crime problem. But if you look carefully at the roofline of any new supercenter, you will see cameras trained on the parking lot. Criminal activity at Wal-Mart stores is not unique — but the company's reaction to these crimes certainly is. In the courtroom, the company has tried to stonewall presentation of the company's records and statistics on crime. Plaintiffs have run into a wall of resistance when they tried to gather evidence of crime at Wal-Mart.

On September 8, 1990, 37-year-old Dorothy McClung's body was found in Crittenden County, Arkansas. Later that day, police apprehended Joseph Alexander Harper II, a 16-year-old from Chattanooga. Harper confessed, in a taped conversation, to abducting Mrs. McClung from the parking lot of a Wal-Mart store in Memphis, Tennessee on September 7, 1990. Harper stated that he abducted Mrs. McClung in her car from the parking lot of a Wal-Mart store located in the Delta Square Shopping Center. McClung's body was found in an Arkansas field by hunters. Joseph Harper was convicted of kidnapping, rape and murder, and hanged himself with a bed sheet after being sentenced to life in jail.

The victim's husband sued Wal-Mart on behalf of himself and his three children. In his suit, he claimed that Wal-Mart and the shopping center were negligent in failing to provide security measures for the parking lot, and that their negligence resulted in his wife's death.

The Tennessee trial court that first heard the case ruled in favor of Wal-Mart, because prior court rulings in the state said that shop owners are not responsible for the criminal acts of third parties unless the owner knew, or should have known, that acts were occurring, or were about to occur that would pose an imminent probability of harm. When the husband appealed to the Tennessee Court of Appeals, the judgement in favor of Wal-Mart was affirmed. The plaintiff then pursued his case to the Tennessee Supreme Court.

In the Supreme Court case, the judge stated that, "Parking lots in particular have provided fertile ground for crime, because customers usually possess money or recently purchased merchandise." She also noted that most courts have ruled that businesses do have a duty to take reasonable precautions to protect customers from foreseeable criminal acts. The judge set a new negligence standard for Tennessee: "The foreseeability of harm and the gravity of harm must be balanced against the commensurate burden imposed on the business to protect against that harm...businesses must justifiably expect to share in the cost of crime attracted to the business."

During the case, McClung's husband presented records from the Memphis Police Department which showed that during a 17-month period leading up to his wife's abduction, 164 criminal incidents had occurred on or near Wal-Mart's parking lot. The crime reports included a bomb threat, 14 burglaries, 12 reports of malicious mischief, 10 robberies, 36 car thefts, 9 larcenies, and 1 attempted kidnapping on an adjacent parking lot. One nearby business even posted guards in five watch towers in its parking lot. The manager of the Wal-Mart store testified that he would not hold sidewalk sales at his store, except for dirt, out of fear the merchandise would be stolen.

In its defense, Wal-Mart argued that the parking lot attack was neither foreseeable nor preventable. The company said that providing security was prohibitively expensive, and had little impact on preventing crime. The plaintiff produced an article written by Dave Gorman,

Wal-Mart's Vice President of Loss Prevention, published in *Security Management* magazine in March 1996. In the article, Gorman boasted that Wal-Mart's security measures in parking lots had produced "outstanding" results: "The survey showed that 80% of crimes at Wal-Mart were occurring not in the stores, but outside their walls, either in the parking lots or in the exterior perimeter of the stores."

In the June 1996 issue of *Parking Security Report*, Gorman admitted, "The biggest issue for us when we first started talking about it was the fact that we were having a lot of crime on the lots. The huge majority of it was crimes against property." After new security measures began, Gorman wrote, "Crime went down dramatically. It just dropped." Gorman further contradicted Wal-Mart's claims in court that security measures were expensive. "The cost of doing it wasn't quite as expensive as what we had been doing. So we saved a little money and did much more effective work."

On October 28, 1996, the Tennessee Supreme Court ruled that the risk of injury to the plaintiff's wife was reasonably foreseeable, and that a jury could conclude that Wal-Mart's negligence was a substantial factor in bringing about the harm. The case was sent back to the Trial Court for a trial by jury. The response from Wal-Mart's lawyer? "Crime is here to stay, unfortunately, and this [ruling] is putting it over on businesses instead of the police department. Are businesses in high crime areas going to be required to put an army outside their door?"

Five years later, on a *60 Minutes* broadcast on January 7, 2001, Danny Hardin, a former security manager at the Memphis, Tennessee store where Dorothy McClung was kidnapped, admitted he had warned his company that they needed to augment security. In a videotaped deposition, Hardin said under oath that Wal-Mart had not only known about the crime problem, it had ignored his requests for additional security:

> HARDIN: We also talked about putting cameras, outside cameras, on top of the building. We talked about patrols in the parking lot.
> 60 MINUTES (voiceover): When asked why his advice was ignored, he said a Wal-Mart vice president told him...
> HARDIN: We did not want to project an image that we needed security.

But Wal-Mart desperately needed security in July 1996 when a woman named Donna Meissner claimed she was abducted from a Wal-Mart parking lot in Jefferson County, Texas. In her complaint against Wal-Mart, Meissner's lawyer, Alto Watson, wrote, "Donna Meissner had no idea that her life would be unalterably changed upon her going to Wal-Mart [where she] was abducted from behind by an assailant with a weapon, forced into an automobile, taken from the premises, brutally raped, had her life threatened and for reasons known only to God, was let go by her assailant."

Meissner sued Wal-Mart for "premises liability" and for not taking the steps necessary to protect customers in the parking lot. During the "discovery" phase of the case, Meissner's attorney attempted to get Wal-Mart to produce a copy of a the Wal-Mart security report from 1993, which showed that 80% of Wal-Mart crimes occur in parking lots. The company never produced the report, and the judge in the case, James Mehaffy, levied an $18 million sanction fine against Wal-Mart for discovery abuse. The judge told reporters, "I hope the stockholders do learn about this, and I hope some pressure is applied to Wal-Mart to make it behave as a responsible corporate citizen."

One of the top Wal-Mart lawyers later admitted that the company deserved to be punished, because it did not comply with the letter and the spirit of Texas discovery rules. "Wal-Mart is engaging in a searching re-evaluation of the litigation processes which have led the parties to this courtroom on this day," said Wal-Mart lawyer Ron Williams. "Wal-Mart recognizes and affirms its obligations to comply with the letter and the spirit of the appropriate rules of procedure concerning discovery matters." The lawyer apologized to Donna Meissner and her lawyers, and said Wal-Mart "regrets the misguided conduct that has brought us here today."

The Meissner lawsuit against Wal-Mart was settled, and the terms of the settlement were confidential. It is unknown what level of financial compensation Wal-Mart paid Meissner, and whether or not the public apology from Wal-Mart was part of the deal. The judge, however, never signed the order for Wal-Mart to pay the $18 million fine, so Wal-Mart was never punished for withholding information. Meissner's lawyer claimed that Wal-Mart should have turned over documents relating to as many as thirty lawsuits against the company for inadequate security. When Wal-Mart was fined, they appealed the decision all the way to the

Texas Supreme Court, which let the lower court ruling stand.

Lawyers who bring suits against Wal-Mart refer to the company as "an obstructionist company" because it has a track record of not producing information requested by courts during the discovery phase of a lawsuit. Such delays cause plaintiffs time and money, and obstruct justice. Meissner's lawyer, Alto Watson, told the court that Wal-Mart had "systematically engaged in a conspiracy to withhold information from victims who have been injured at their stores relating to a lack of security statewide." He called Wal-Mart's behavior "simply reprehensible...There is not an adequate adjective or adverb to describe it other than 'criminal.'"

A story in the *National Law Journal* reported that May 25, 2000 was a "bad day in court for Wal-Mart Stores, Inc." First, the company admitted to "misguided conduct" in a Texas rape/abduction case, and then, in a case from Illinois, a District Court judge said the company's witness had "lied to cover Wal-Mart's tracks." After months of court hearings in this case, a Wal-Mart employee claimed that he had never seen the 1993-94 Wal-Mart study of crime committed on store properties, despite evidence that he had seen the report in 1997. The Illinois judge said the Wal-Mart witness was lying about his knowledge of his company's crime reports, which had been written about in two trade magazines. "I do believe that he lied to cover Wal-Mart's tracks," the judge said. He added that Wal-Mart's Vice President for Loss Prevention was "considerably less than candid" when he testified that the company did not keep records of criminal acts in its stores for more than 30 days. The Judge found that a wholly owned Wal-Mart subsidiary, CMI, compiles crime data for the company. The Judge ordered Wal-Mart CEO Lee Scott to appear before him to answer whether Wal-Mart's "discovery compliance deficiencies" were the result of company policy.

Given this court history, it is understandable that Wal-Mart doesn't like to talk about crime inside or outside its stores. One former Wal-Mart security guard described crime prevention measures taken at his store:

> Surveillance is predominantly with cameras, but it is a known fact, they are watching the associates, not the crooks. They [the cameras] are not real good quality, and the focal capabilities are not that great.

They're there to have people believe they are safe, and signs posted everywhere state that. The "crooks" know they won't prosecute after the fact, and don't care if they're on them or not. In the parking lot, all you can see are shapes, and hardly ever enough to describe a person or thing. Security is two-fold. The first is outside, which is at best, "casual observance," designed to discourage, and fairly effective, as nothing has been stolen since I had been there, and the incidents of accidents, etc, have been settled, or solved effectively. The second is Loss Prevention, LP, or "in-store," who meander around, as unobtrusive as possible, directly observing behavior, and apprehending shoplifters, from time to time, again, as example. The directive had been, according to home office, no stop — except by Loss Prevention or Management. Further, no confrontation. Their idea of liability control. I've had people, seen shoplifting valuable merchandise, walk right out, right by me, and could do nothing. It's window dressing, and the management are not taught anything related to theft, or shoplifting, so cooperation is non-existent. Whenever an incident did occur, management was "lost," so the Police were always called, and could do little, because either they didn't see it, or the incident was long over before they arrived.

Even though Wal-Mart may not want to project an image that it needs security, some communities now project the public safety costs of a mall on their local budget, and factor in the added cost of increased police patrols at shopping centers. Typical of such calculations are these findings from Economic & Planning Systems, a Berkeley, California land use consultant:

> A recent fiscal analysis conducted by EPS of a major new regional shopping center in the Bay Area indicated that the local police department reported an average of 50 calls for service per month, or about 1.5 calls per 1,000 square feet of retail space annually after the shopping center opened for business.

Taxpayers are realizing that big box stores can mean big public safety expenditures. In Murphy, Texas, during a public hearing on a proposed Wal-Mart in August 1999, residents complained about

potential traffic, delivery trucks, and the impact on city services —
especially the police. "I like to have the police riding down the street,"
one resident testified. "I don't feel the police should be sitting in parking
lots protecting the interests of a big corporation like Wal-Mart."

Several years ago, I had coffee with the Chief of Police in
Tappahannock, Virginia. I asked him to tell me what he thought about
the 24-hour Wal-Mart that had opened in his small town in the Northern
Neck of Virginia. He told me that police records in Tappahannock
indicate that the supercenter has been responsible for 21% of all criminal
offense records over the past 21 months in that community. "It's been a
drain on our resources," he said. The chief told me he would be happy to
see the store close and move to some other location. He said the major
mistake was letting the store stay open all night. People gather there at
night because there are very few other places to go.

Citizens in Mesa, Arizona who were battling a Wal-Mart sent me
a report from the Chandler, Arizona police department. It's a "call type
summary" of police reports from one address: 800 W. Warner Road, the
Wal-Mart location. The police report shows that in 1998 there was a total
of 434 police summons to the Wal-Mart, including the following reports:

| Call Description | Call Total |
|---|---|
| Accident/non-injury/hit and run | 11 |
| Disorderly Conduct | 11 |
| Forged Checks | 63 |
| Shoplifter in custody | 101 |
| Shoplifter combative | 8 |
| Theft Report | 24 |

In Chandler, residents got more than low, everyday Wal-Mart
prices. They got everyday police calls as well. The police log in
Chandler includes a narcotics report, a sex offense, domestic fights,
found juvenile, indecent exposure, mentally disturbed person, missing
juvenile — everything from abandoned vehicles to bomb threats. A total
of 434 police calls. When public officials in Chandler formed a chorus
to welcome Wal-Mart to their community, they probably did not give a

second thought to the cost of supporting a huge, 24/7 retail facility.

The incidence of Wal-Mart-related crime in Chandler is not an anomaly. A search of police reports in Rohnert Park, California over a 17-month period shows that police had to respond to 614 calls, or more than one call daily to the Wal-Mart plaza. Ninety reports resulted in arrests. There can be a very significant public cost to this concentrated police activity.

An article in May 2002 in the *St. Petersburg Times* in Florida illustrates how petty crimes at Wal-Mart can add up to a high price tag for local authorities. Wal-Mart has a policy of pressing charges on shoplifting incidents. In Port Richey, which has a population just over 3,000, the *St. Petersburg Times* reported that crime at Wal-Mart "meant a lot of work for the city's 14 member police force." The newspaper claimed that police in Port Richey take longer to respond to other calls for assistance, have to work overtime schedules, perform less traffic patrols, and may need to hire more officers. Chief of Police William Downs told the paper that his men were often tied up processing shoplifters at Wal-Mart. If Wal-Mart calls to report a shoplifting, the police have to respond. Because two officers go out on every call for safety reasons, when someone is arrested at Wal-Mart, the city's only police are at the store. "Our response times are, in some cases, slower," the chief said. "Our calls are backed up now more than ever before."

The *St. Petersburg Times* produced a study that showed the monthly averages for minor citizen incidents climbed after Wal-Mart arrived. In the year before Wal-Mart opened, police never took longer than eight minutes to respond to a drunken pedestrian call. In the year after Wal-Mart opened, they took as long as fifty-one minutes to respond. Police tied up at Wal-Mart are not able to issue tickets. In a ten-month period in 2000, the police wrote 2,069 traffic or parking tickets. But in the 10 months after Wal-Mart opened, they wrote just about half – 1,077.

Shoplifting cases can tie up police for hours. The incidents at Wal-Mart included children left unattended in cars, domestic disputes, and trespassing. Chief Downs warns other communities, "You might want to consider additional personnel, otherwise your other areas of services may suffer."

The Port Richey Wal-Mart pays the town $75,000 a year in property taxes. The Chief, who has a staff of fourteen, asked the town for two more officers and got one. He has also been forced to pay out mandatory overtime to his staff. In the budget year that began October 2001, Port Richey earmarked $22,180 for police overtime. But by April 2002, with five months left in the fiscal year, the city had spent $72,275 on overtime. The newspaper's study reveals that nearly one in four people arrested in Port Richey from March through December 2001 was arrested at Wal-Mart. From the day it opened, Wal-Mart accounted for 1 out of every 16 calls to the police. In one 10-month period, the police were summoned to Wal-Mart more than 400 times. Because of all this activity, Chief Downs had to ask Port Richey for two new officers, which would cost the town nearly $54,000 for salaries alone.

In researching their story, the *St. Petersburg Times* recorded Wal-Mart impacts in other communities. In Beloit, Wisconsin, Wal-Mart gave the police space for a substation inside its store — so they could cut down on travel time from the police station to the retailer. In North Versailles, Pennsylvania, Wal-Mart police incidents caused the police force to grow from 10 to 26 officers over a four-year period.

According to the *St. Petersburg Times*, the Wal-Mart manager of the Port Richey, Florida store "scoffed at" the idea that Wal-Mart should underwrite some of the cost of these added police expenses. "As a citizen and a taxpayer," the Wal-Mart manager told the paper, "I expect them to take care of my needs."

The needs of Wal-Mart's customers take a back seat to the corporation's need to limit its liability in court. The company's legal resources are often brought to bear against the victims of crime at Wal-Mart. Despite the history of criminal incidents on its premises, highly publicized lawsuits from customers, and the nation's hyper-sensitivity to community violence in the post-Columbine High School period, Wal-Mart seems to react indifferently to criticism of its role as the largest private seller of guns and ammunition in the world. A grocer in Minnesota emailed me a photograph that some people might consider a sick joke. It was an in-store display from a Wal-Mart with a sign that read, "Back 2 School." The price below the sign read $15.58.

On the display was a pile of products in cardboard boxes, with some of the contents opened and stacked upon the boxes. The product was branded with a big "Federal" marked on the side, with a sticker below it that read, "Value Pack." I couldn't tell from the photo what the product was, so I emailed my correspondent back.

"What's the item in the box?" I asked him. "I don't recognize that brand name. What kind of school supply is that?"

The reply came back: "Those are boxes of shotgun shells."

# Count 13:
# Injurious to Private Property

*"We want people to know that having a Wal-Mart*
*in your neighborhood is a good thing."*
-Lee Scott, Wal-Mart CEO, Annual Stockholders Meeting, June 6, 2003

It's important for Wal-Mart to project the image of being a good neighbor. But a store 4 or 5 times the size of a football field presents unique challenges to any residential community.

Dee Brantley lives in a modest home in Lake Charles, Louisiana, with her husband Robert. They have lived at their residence for the past eleven years, surrounded by a backyard that Dee describes as "a welcoming retreat, bordered by thickly forested wetlands with abundant wildlife."

That's the backyard. But in the front yard of her home, is a lawn sign that reads:

HELP!
We are P.O.W.s
(Prisoners of Wal-Mart)
Victims of Bentonvillains
& local indifference to our suffering

Dee is one of 18 homeowners in her community who have filed a lawsuit against Wal-Mart, its developer and the construction company that put up a supercenter in their backyards. The petition for damages, filed in the 14th District Court, claims that the defendants intentionally misrepresented their plans to neighbors as an office park.

This effectively silenced any opposition from neighboring residents to the annexation, rezoning, and development of the property through repeated assurances that the development of the subject property would not offend neighboring residents.

"The developer's original plan that he showed us," Dee said, "had absolutely no Wal-Mart. It was to be an office park/strip mall, small shops, etc. There was no indication of a Wal-Mart."

During construction of the Wal-Mart, Dee was forced to seek refuge from the 24-hour-a-day construction noise by sleeping in her bedroom closet. The project has caused major flooding in her home on at least four occasions. "The noise and diesel fumes never stop," Dee says. "You wouldn't treat an animal this way."

When Wal-Mart began building its supercenter — much to the surprise of neighbors — everything in the neighborhood began to change. "The construction phase was absolute torture," Dee says. "The dirt work was relentless, pounding and more pounding. The backhoes, the bulldozers, the helicopters, the cranes, the diesel fumes and dust swirled in clouds so thick and hot you could barely see or breathe." This went on for months. "The trees were cut down," Dee adds, "and the lot remained vacant for two years."

Dirt leveling on the site began in July 2000 and it was an absolute nightmare. Dee's 5-feet by 7-feet window shattered from construction vibration. An open ditch 680 feet long and 5 feet deep remained open with no fencing for at least three and a half months. "I came home and there was this huge 'Grand Canyon.' No safety netting, no fence, no barrier," Dee recalls. "I had to sleep in my closet for a week solid and board up my windows inside and out with plywood to get relief from generators being allowed to run all night. They're still running all night, and the city does nothing. The politicians expect us to pay their salaries in the form of our taxes, while we have to sleep in our closets."

The Brantley's home flooded after the Wal-Mart was developed. Their once beautiful backyard now floods, and their property has significantly depreciated in value. Their legal complaint charges that Wal-Mart ignored residents' complaints and chose to run its 24-hour, 7-day-a-week store with little or no regard for its neighbors. The developer leveled a 25-acre wooded area, removing every tree or blade of grass to the limit of the property line. The natural flow of rainfall was altered and some homes and yards were flooded. Neighbors are now constantly harassed and disturbed by the sight and sound of 18-wheelers and other vehicles at all hours of the day and night. The lawsuit claims homeowners have lost their enjoyment of property, suffered depreciation of value and property damage, mental distress and harassment.

For Dee Brantley and her neighborhood in Lake Charles, when the Wal-Martians landed, their community became a hell on earth. The Mayor of Lake Charles consoled the neighbors by suggesting that once the outside work on the superstore was over, their complaints would subside. "You probably won't even know they are there when the work starts inside," the Mayor said. But the torment never stopped. Today Dee still signs her letters "Wal-Mart P.O.W."

"Whenever these Wal-Mart people tell me that they're just trying to make a living, " Dee says. "I just tell them 'We're just trying to make a life — and we were here first. I don't know where Mr. Lee Scott [Wal-Mart's CEO] lives, but I'd be willing to wager that it's not right next to a 24/7 Wal-Mart superstore. I've yet to know one of them that is willing to live next door to one of these monsters."

Unfortunately, Dee Brantley's neighborhood speaks for many communities across the country that were caught completely off-guard when Wal-Mart's bulldozers showed up. If you walk into Nathan and Lisa Murphy's living room in the Somerset subdivision in Charlotte, North Carolina, voices echo off the bare walls. There is no furniture in the room, nothing at all. The Murphys paid $257,000 for the 3,000-square-foot, two-story brick home Lisa calls her dream house.

But the dream became a nightmare.

Somerset subdivision was pitched to potential homeowners as a "master-planned community." It was advertised as "majestic in nature." The developers had set aside 20% of the land area for open space. There were preserved wetlands, walking trails, and fairly low county taxes. The Stone Crest shopping center was only a 10-minute drive.

The Murphys found out in November 2001 that Wal-Mart planned to build a 206,000-square-foot, 24-hour supercenter directly behind their house near the corner of Rea and Tom Short Roads. Nathan found out about his new neighbor quite by accident. He was working at home when he noticed a yellow bulldozer clearing the land just beyond his fence. Nathan went back to the tree-filled lot and asked a couple of people who were standing there what was going on.

"The guys said, 'Yeah, they're putting up a Wal-Mart,'" Nathan recalls. "One guy said, 'I was just looking at those houses and thinking, how tragic.'"

Nathan then told him: "I live in that house."

Nathan immediately called Lisa at the Charlotte branch of the Bank of America, where she worked. Lisa was stunned by the news and took the rest of the day off. "Just looking at the plans made me start bawling," Lisa told a local reporter.

The Murphys had moved to Charlotte just six months earlier from Lake Wylie, South Carolina. They made the move because they wanted a bigger house in which to raise their three children and a better school system. They knew that the 30 acres located behind them was zoned commercial — but the developer had assured them that the field was largely wetlands, and could only sustain a small project, like a church or day care center.

What they got instead was a proposal for a Wal-Mart supercenter.

Instead of the planned unit development they bought into, the Murphys were now slated to live with Wal-Mart as a nightlight.

Lisa began organizing the neighborhood. She made up some fliers to distribute in mailboxes, and arranged for a neighborhood meeting. Initially, no one believed Lisa's story about the supercenter, but the group quickly coalesced into the Citizens for Smart Growth. They began raising money to fight the world's largest retailer and retained a lawyer.

The Murphys' first move was to challenge a Union County zoning administrator's ruling that the Wal-Mart parcel was exempt from a zoning ordinance that limited store size to 120,000 square feet. But the county Board of Adjustment ruled that even though retail buildings on land zoned B-2 were capped at 120,000 square feet, the county had given the developers permission to develop it under previous rules, and the Murphys had missed the deadline for filing an appeal. The county's land use plan called for "neighborhood-scaled" shopping.

Lisa quit her job at the bank to free up more time to research the legal issues surrounding the case. Her home gradually filled up with plastic crates full of land use ordinances, engineering maps, and North Carolina zoning statutes. She was spending 30 to 40 hours a week amassing information.

Lisa found discrepancies over how much of Wal-Mart's land could actually be developed commercially and how the land had been developed over the years. She found the original Master Plan for her subdivision folded up in a pile of documents in the county attorney's office. Her research gave county officials the background they needed at least temporarily to hold off giving Wal-Mart any project permits. The case pivots on definitions found in the zoning code. The Murphys argue that Wal-Mart is a "shopping center" under the code, and is subject to the size cap. Wal-Mart says they are a "department store" and are not limited by size. Either way, the project has to obtain a special use permit, show that it will not harm surrounding properties, and that it is consistent with the county's land use plan. "It took me too long to realize that all the hollering and screaming wouldn't get us anywhere," Lisa admits. "It was all in the zoning."

But the neighbors have been left in limbo. A Wal-Mart spokesman said the company was committed to building a ten-foot sound wall behind the superstore, plus extra landscaping and screening. He suggested that the company might even ask its architects for a "unique design, not your off-the-shelf Wal-Mart," according to a local newspaper. But the Murphys point out that the superstore will be in the worst possible location in their planned unit development. "The dumpsters for this store will be directly across the street from a family with five children," Lisa notes.

Once word about the Wal-Mart spread throughout the larger community, sales of new homes in the undeveloped portion of Somerset dropped dramatically. As of January 2003, 35 lots remained unsold, and three buyers actually backed out of their deals. "It's a very unfortunate thing for us," admits the president of the home construction company building the units, "and for the homeowners."

Lisa, in the meantime, has started her own internet company. She says she never could have kept working at the bank and still carried on her campaign. Her legal wrangling with Wal-Mart is only getting started. "There are lawsuits all over the place," she says. "We have enough legal grounds to keep this going."

After almost two years of battles, Lisa says her energy is still strong. "Whenever I go down to the county offices I take along with me a picture of my kids. And I put the picture on the table and tell them,

'This is why I'm here.' I'm not doing this for the fun of it. I'm scared."

Lisa says her living room and dining room still have no furniture in them, and she's held off from doing any landscaping on the property. "I'm not going to throw a lot of money into this house until this gets settled," she explains.

Using a pledge system, Lisa has raised $60,000 from her neighbors since this fight began. "I'm $10,000 in debt right now," Lisa admits, "but the pledges are doing really well."

When asked about her relationship with Wal-Mart, Lisa just laughs.

"They had a lot of guts walking right into the middle of this development like they did," Lisa says. "They're a ruthless company."

Nowhere is this ruthlessness towards neighborhoods more pronounced than in the St. Louis suburb of Maplewood, Missouri, population 9,200.

Homeowners in Maplewood contacted me in August 2002 out of growing desperation:

> Our city council passed two ordinances over a year ago to blight 122 homes, 12 existing businesses, a church and a 16-unit apartment complex to make way for a Wal-Mart and Sam's Club. The original developer, PACE Properties, dropped out due to pressure from the residents in the buy-out area who decided they wanted THF Realty as the developer because THF was going to offer more money for their homes. A small group of residents, located in the buy-out area, decided to fight. We obtained enough signatures to force a referendum.
>
> Those of us who decided to fight feel like we are sinking. We have been maligned, threatened, etc. by the residents in the buy-out and these residents have joined forces with the city. City officials, who claim the city is broke, sought an injunction to have a special election on Sept. 17th, but we found out that the city did not disclose information to the judge. We are filing a law suit tomorrow with the Board of Election Commission trying to change the election date to Nov. 3. The city has broken the sunshine law several times and we are trying to address that through the courts. It's a mess. We are also trying to hold weekly meetings for the residents to have an open forum to discuss this, but our first meeting last week resulted in the

buy-out people crashing the meeting, banging on the door and a group were led into the back with our city's mayor. They remained disruptive throughout the meeting. We are holding another meeting this Wednesday, trying again, but think people are afraid to come.

The developer THF managed to win a development contract from the city of Maplewood by out-bidding another developer. THF got more homeowners in the affected area to sell out to them than their rival — enticing homeowners with a $1,000 sign-on bonus. When some residents refused to be bought out, and gathered nearly 1,000 signatures to put the retail project to a voter's referendum, THF responded by donating $125,000 to the YES committee.

According to Missouri Ethics Commission financial reports, the YES group received 99.6% of its money from THF. With that money, the pro-development group spent $8,700 on a public opinion poll, $35,500 on a telemarketing campaign, $12,500 on campaign staff, $31,527 on printing, and $2,895 on yard signs. During the month of September alone, THF spent $95,286 on the campaign — a rate of $3,811 every day of the 25-day reporting period.

The citizens against the rezoning raised less than $8,000, or 6% of THF's corporate contributions. The residents fighting for their homes were outspent 16 to 1. To make matters worse, local residents discovered that "Sam's Club in the city of St. Louis is closing when the Maplewood store is being opened less than 3 miles away and Wal-Mart is reneging on their commitment to the St. Louis City Market Place Shopping Center, which will still owe $10 million in bond monies until 2011, even though this shopping center is withering away."

There is a strong dose of corporate welfare to swallow in Maplewood. The developer and Wal-Mart stood to gain from a $16 million taxpayer gift called the Transportation Development District. The money is raised by a 1% sales tax on all goods sold in this development, and the money is used to help construct the necessary infrastructure for the benefit of the developer. Missouri shoppers will put up the money to subsidize the world's largest retailer.

Shortly before the election, the homeowners of Maplewood nervously wrote me: "It is 6 days from the election and things are very stressful as you can imagine. We are very concerned about the outcome. Unfortunately, it seems Wal-Mart has bought the votes. The development has been endorsed by our city, the school district, the local business association and endorsed by the *St. Louis Post Dispatch*. It's really a joke."

The conclusion was foregone. You could hear the bulldozer engines revving up as election day arrived. Ron Mink, an organizer of the anti-Wal-Mart effort, sent me the following email:

> We are sorry to have to report that we lost the election on November 5th. Maplewood, Missouri will have a Wal-Mart/Sam's. The vote was about 2:1 for blighting 33 acres and having THF build a Wal-Mart and Sam's. We were outspent and unfortunately, we couldn't get the residents who didn't want the development (1000 people who voted no) to help. Wal-Mart contributed $125,000 to their campaign and the unions contributed about $15,000 to our campaign. Plus, we didn't get the money in a timely way. We have heard that all the contracts have expired, so it should be interesting to see if THF honors them at the original price. I seriously doubt it, and we'll probably get blamed for that.

Mayor Mark Langston of Maplewood, Missouri told reporters he was "really pleased" that a Wal-Mart and Sam's Club were given the green light by voters. THF had approval to bulldoze an entire neighborhood of 150 homes. The Mayor's cavalier response in the *St. Louis Post Dispatch* was: "We hate to lose these folks, but they're getting a good price for their homes."

Mayor Langston attributed the falling revenues in town to the $400,000 in sales tax lost when Kmart shut its doors three years ago. The Mayor had to choose between the 150 families in Maplewood and Wal-Mart — the very company that had already caused the town to lose revenue and cut several town workers. The Mayor chose Wal-Mart. It was the Mayor's political decision that Maplewood had only two choices: raise revenues from retail sales, or raise property taxes. "We decided not to raise property taxes," the Mayor painfully admitted, "but unfortunately we had to get rid of 150 homes. They're not houses — they're homes. We're going to miss those families. That's the bitter part of the pill." But to the Mayor of Maplewood, it all comes down to dollars and cents: "We're all pretty happy that they're being compensated well."

"I'm glad we're not raising taxes," Langston said. "I think that's great." The Mayor described the loss of 150 families as "a sacrifice of the few for the many here."

After the vote, Ron Mink told me: "The neighborhood that I live in, the home that I occupy, will forever be changed. It's with a great sadness that all of us will now have to face a future of finding new homes."

There were still some homeowners who refused to sign contracts to sell to THF Realty. But if they don't accept Wal-Mart's price, the town will then condemn their homes and give them a "fair market" price. A number of businesses in the area also refused to sell out to THF. Mayor Langston made it clear the next move was his: "If we need to blight them and move them on with a fair price, that's what we'll do."

About one week after the election, THF announced that it planned to expand its retail empire beyond just the Wal-Mart and Sam's Club, to open a Lowe's home improvement store, razing another 52 homes in a residential area, bringing the total homes destroyed to more than 200. THF also wants state taxpayers to give him corporate welfare to tear down the homes, in the form of Tax Incremental Financing (TIF), a form of state tax breaks.

In Maplewood, Wal-Mart took down an entire community. The corporation's needs were more important than the neighborhood that 200 families called home. Houses began coming down in 2003.

As Maplewood was falling, a group of residents in Henderson, Kentucky were fighting a similar battle for survival. It was their third battle against a Wal-Mart proposal. The company first announced plans to construct a superstore in the thick of a densely populated Henderson housing subdivision. One of the neighbors, Pamela Thomas, wrote a local reporter about the "neighbor from hell" syndrome. In her letter, she mentioned Doc Campbell, one of her neighbors. "Doc is one of the most honest and intelligent people I have ever met. He and his wife Judy have lived at the corner of Taransay and Bannockburn for more than two decades." The back of the Campbell's home overlooks the Wal-Mart property. "I would like to ask the present mayor, the ex–mayor, the developer's attorney, and the landowner to consider buying and living in Doc Campbell's home for the next 10 years," Thomas wrote. "Or how about Rick and Marlene Curby's home? Or Garland and Betty Bingemer's home on 60 East? In each of these three homes, each located on a different side of the development, the mayor, ex-mayor, developer's attorney, and the landowner will get a good, well-lighted view of their beautiful 55-acre, 24-hour shopping center. Either that, or they could approve such a development next to their present homes. I bet even the developer does not live next to his development in Brentwood, Tennessee."

In the fall of 2003, two lawsuits were filed against the developer and the city to challenge the Henderson Wal-Mart, and the court challenges could slow the project down for another year or two.

Henderson. Maplewood. Charlotte. Lake Charles. The homeowners in these communities — and dozens of others around the country — know first-hand about Wal-Mart's "good neighbor" policy. If they had known about it far enough in advance, they might have found a way to escape their "good neighbor" before they became trapped. But now they are in court, or hiding in their closet, or wherever neighbors go to avoid the reality of a daily confrontation with Wal-Mart.

Wal-Mart can build stores called "Neighborhood Markets." But they cannot build neighborhoods. There is no such thing as a "Wal-Mart neighborhood." It is a contradiction in terms.

# Instructions to the Jury:
# A Shoppers' Boycott

*"It will be a sad day in this country if we wake up one morning and
all we find is a Wal-Mart on every corner."*
—Gary Hawkins, Green Hills Supermarket, Syracuse, NY
as quoted in *Business Week* magazine, October 2003

All across the country, when local residents stand up at public
hearings to challenge the rampant "developer-take-all" attitude, they
are met with incredulity and downright anger. "Who are *you* to tell me
where to shop?" It's as if collectively we have come to believe that
there is really such a thing as A Constitutional Right to Shop. It comes
somewhere after Life, Liberty and the Pursuit of Cheap Underwear. Woe
to anyone who attempts to trample on that Right To Shop.

In June 2003, frustrated residents of Brattleboro, Vermont
organized a group called BrattPower to encourage local consumers to
shop local and avoid big box stores. A spokesman for the developer
described the boycott as "bizarre," and claimed that his company rarely
encountered opposition when it comes to a community. "At the least,"
the spokesman said, "this is most undemocratic. People ought to have
the right to shop and not shop where they choose, and not have someone
impose their beliefs on them."

There is a sense of shopping entitlement, both at the consumer
level, and inside the corporate culture of big box stores. This entitlement
is expressed in a bumper sticker I saw:

"OUTTA MY WAY I'M SHOPPING AT WAL-MART!"

An incident in Orange City, Florida made national headlines the day after Thanksgiving 2003. On "Black Friday," when retailers start to emerge from red ink into profitability, Wal-Mart announced that it had recorded more than $1.5 billion in sales that day — more than most small retailers see in a year. The media carried stories and photos of shoppers pushing and shoving their way to the biggest bargains. In Orange City, Wal-Mart shoppers scrambled for everyday low prices on a DVD player. In the stampede, a 41-year-old woman named Patricia VanLester, who was first in line to buy a $29 DVD player, ended up in the hospital instead, when the crowd knocked her to the ground. "They walked over her like a herd of elephants," the woman's sister told the *Associated Press*. "I told them, 'Stop stepping on my sister. She's on the ground.' All they cared about was a stupid DVD player."

When paramedics arrived, they found the injured shopper unconscious, lying on top of a cheap DVD player. The woman was flown to a hospital in Daytona Beach, where doctors told the media VanLester had suffered a seizure after she was knocked down. "Patty doesn't remember anything," her sister said. "She still can't believe it all happened." A spokesperson for the retailer said she had never heard of such a fight for a sale item. "We are very disappointed this happened," the spokesperson said. "We want her to come back as a shopper." Wal-Mart offered to put a DVD player on hold for her.

Who was the victim here? VanLester's sister was correct: "All they cared about was a stupid DVD." But then, VanLester had put herself in harm's way — standing in line in front of a herd of elephants at Wal-Mart at 6 a.m. just to save a few bucks on an electronic gadget. VanLester was just another of the shoppers who helped Wal-Mart reach its $1.5 billion record sales figure on Black Friday. It was almost over VanLester's dead body that this new sales height was reached. In all likelihood, VanLester went back later to Wal-Mart to get her "stupid DVD." After all, it was on hold for her.

Shopping is no longer a casual, recreational activity. Going to the superstore has been elevated to a patriotic act. The state of the economy is portrayed as dependent not on production, but on consumption — what the economists call "consumer confidence." The way a loyal American helps his or her country is by spending. Every calendar quarter, the sales figures from major retailers are measured and analyzed by Wall Street investment firms. Wal-Mart's "same store sales" have become the tea leaves for economic prognosticators. Linking national well-being with household consumption has been going on since the post-World War II era, but never before has the barometer of economic activity been so focused on how many Barbie dolls are sold at Wal-Mart.

As Americans, we have specific rights that are enumerated under the amendments to the U.S. Constitution: the right to a fair trial, the right to bear arms, the right to equal protection under the law, the right to petition government for a redress of grievances, and so on. I have been using my First Amendment rights to slow down the spread of Wal-Marts, Home Depots, and Targets into every little village and hamlet in North America. Developers may be correct that zoning is nothing more than a set of "beliefs," but such beliefs are rooted in state law and the local power of communities to guide their own destiny and determine their landscape and environment.

There are apparently many Americans who believe they have a constitutional Right to Shop. To hear some of these folks talk, there is a 28th Amendment for Shopper's Rights. These people tend to show up at planning board and zoning board hearings wearing yellow Mr. Smiley buttons whenever a Wal-Mart applies to locate anywhere within shouting distance of their home. I don't know where they go the rest of the time, but a Wal-Mart or a Target hearing brings them to City Hall. They are exercising their First Amendment rights, but they think they are exercising their unwritten 28th Amendment Right To Shop.

This misconception over a Right to Shop has been encouraged by corporations that seem equally confused. When Wal-Mart tried to rezone waterfront property in Eureka, California from industrial to commercial in 1999, they produced literature that told residents the fight was all about "your right to shop at Wal-Mart." The "right to rezoning" seemed too abstract — but a "right to shop" hit closer to home.

In the Eureka case, Wal-Mart hired a law firm from San Francisco to draft a four-page legislative document entitled "Citizens' Right to Vote on a Wal-Mart in Eureka." It was actually a detailed zoning amendment, hiding behind the rhetoric of "citizens' rights." Wal-Mart itself put this question on the ballot in Eureka claiming "an initiative is the most fair and democratic process available for the people of Eureka."

The battle was not about the Right to Shop, it was about rezoning land — but if the world's largest retail corporation was confused, what could we expect from the poor, misguided consumer? Wal-Mart took the next five months and spent $235,000 on a voter campaign that they ultimately lost by a 61% to 39% margin. The fact that Wal-Mart was defeated when Eureka residents exercised their right to vote suggests that Wal-Mart's constitutional call to protect "your right to shop" was not a compelling argument.

At a hearing in my hometown of Greenfield, Massachusetts, a warehouse club applied to open a gas station inside its parking lot. I testified that a gas station inside a busy parking lot was a terrible land use precedent, placing pedestrians and cars in conflict. One woman got up and told the Town Council, "I don't think these people should have the right to tell me where I can or can't shop. This is America. I have the right to get gas anywhere I want."

The notion that this citizen/shopper had a right to get gas anywhere she wanted challenged about 25 years of zoning history in one sentence. But if Wal-Mart is telling people they have a Right to Shop, many people will believe it, just as they believe in the pantheon of Wal-Mart culture, from the deification of Sam Walton down to its "customer is boss" dictum.

The Right to Shop is enshrined beside the property rights argument. Property rights advocates believe that an individual should have the "right" to do anything they want with their property, no matter what the impact on surrounding property. One woman recently told me that "sustainable development" was a United Nations/communist conspiracy to rob people of their property rights. From this perspective, zoning is a dirty, six-letter word that compromises pure "property rights." Libertarians are not about to be slowed down by something as conspiratorial as the concept of protecting the health, safety and general welfare of townspeople.

There is something uniquely American about standing up in public and telling the world that you need a store the size of three football fields so you can get whipping cream. At a Wal-Mart hearing in Virginia, a woman rose from her chair to complain that a few days before Thanksgiving she was unable to find a carton of whipping cream at her local stores, and she knew that if a Wal-Mart had been nearby, she would have had her whipping cream. I once heard a college student passionately defend the pros of Wal-Mart development, saying, "Where else can I find Lion King wrapping paper?"

These pleas for whipping cream or Lion King wrapping paper appear frivolous, especially against the global backdrop of third world poverty and environmental degradation. Many people in this country have a distorted sense of entitlement, which includes the demand that every town have a super-sized Sprawl-Mart to gratify their every consumer need. Developers and national retailers, always willing to respond to such entitlement, have overbuilt our landscape, opened thousands of stores in excess of the need, and closed hundreds that they simply "outgrew." Wal-Mart engages in excess development by invoking our name as consumers. The Declaration of Shopping begins with the words "We the customer." In our name Wal-Mart has laid waste to hundreds of thousands of acres every year. According to the International Council of Shopping Centers, in 2001 retailers in America closed down 6,000 stores — twice the number down five years earlier. The day after Kmart announced its bankruptcy, Wal-Mart responded by opening 17 stores in a single day across 12 states! This is Freedom to Shop run amok.

We suffer from a bad case of land use schizophrenia in this country. On the one hand, our illness causes us to create romantic fantasies of hometown life in Mayberry, RFD, while on the other hand to permit developers to rezone Aunt Bee's farm. It is called "cash box zoning:" the practice of selling a small town or neighborhood to the developer with the deepest pockets. The Mayor in one town brokers the best property and sales tax deal for his or her constituents, while the Mayor in the next town tries to land an even bigger mall to steal the revenue from the first town. This corporate hopscotch leaves hundreds of towns with dead malls and sagging revenues.

I have a right to shop at any store I want — but I don't have the right to put that store in your backyard, or in your community, at any size I want. I have a constitutional right to try and stop developers from bulldozing my town. Our cities and towns have the right to use their local zoning powers to determine the size, location and use of buildings.

This sense of entitlement — "I'll shop wherever I want" — is part of the arrogance of the Wal-Mart nation. A new Wal-Mart will hold a ribbon-cutting ceremony somewhere in America every 42 hours. Wal-Mart admitted nearly a decade ago that we are in an overbuilt situation.

Ribbon-cuttings today are driven more by the motive of putting others out of business than to serve some market need.

All of this growth has been done in our name, and we are the only ones who can stop it. The corporations themselves are unable to change, because their survival depends on rising stock prices, and their stock prices are dependent on sales growth. The political solution to big box sprawl is to go on what I call "the superstore diet." There are two things that Americans do to excess: eat and shop. It's possible to combat both indulgences at once by going on a superstore diet.

As the ad from BJ's Wholesale Club says, "You are what you buy." When we shop, we are doing much more than just making a purchase. We're making an investment. We have the choice to invest in a business that respects our community or one that is bent on milking it dry. If we use our income to invest in companies that are wasting our hometown, then we've made a bad investment. Wal-Mart appeals to you as a customer. My appeal to you is as a citizen. If everything we buy is an investment, what kind of a company are we investing in when we make a shopping trip to Wal-Mart?

The decision to shop at a superstore like Wal-Mart may seem like a personal decision — but it affects an entire community. Overstuffed retail giants dominate the economic and social life of small towns, turning them into homogenized, faceless sprawlvilles. The superstores have demonstrated over the last few years that they are increasingly unwilling to modify their behavior to meet local standards of acceptability.

When *The New York Times* asked me to react to the bankruptcy of toy retailer FAO Schwartz just before Christmas 2003, I said, "In Wal-Mart's defense, it is Wal-Mart shoppers who are killing FAO, not Wal-Mart. Wal-Mart is not the beginning of competition, but the end of competition." We cannot blame Wal-Mart for our own shopping decisions. No one is forcing us to shop there. My focus has turned from the *company* to the *customer*. My hope is that an educated consumer is an activated consumer. The more people learn about Wal-Mart as a corporation, the less they will like. Wal-Mart is the most popular store in America, and the most reviled store in America.

We can see all around us the destruction that follows Wal-Mart. In my hometown, there are no Wal-Marts—but there are no other discount competitors either. We are encircled by Wal-Marts in other towns. The other regional retail chains have died, and their empty stores have been filled by the giant retailers who killed them. But we, the consumer, pulled the trigger. We killed competition.

In the same fashion, as consumers we control the future growth of companies like Wal-Mart. The bottom line for megastores is sales revenue. As shoppers, all of us have the right and the ability to make a statement about what we value in our community by choosing where we take our business. Will we continue to invest in companies that disinvest in our communities? Will we fatten the companies that pursue a scorched earth policy against our own neighborhoods? Is our quality of life worth more than a cheap pair of underwear?

We have become a nation of binge shoppers, consuming Barbie dolls and coffee filters as if there were no tomorrow. A psychologist might argue that as our lives become emptier, our shelves become fuller. Our profligate shopping has given Wal-Mart bragging rights for years. The company's 1996 Annual Report boasted that every man, woman and child in America spent an average of $360 at Wal-Mart. They sold us 1,851,000,000 coffee filters that year, 227,592,400 clothespins, and a Barbie doll every two seconds!

Its time for weaning. We are in a unique position to go on a Superstore Diet. It involves no special preparation, no patches or medications, no diet books, no exercise tapes. In August 2003 the National Center for Smart Growth at the University of Maryland reported that the average American living in an area of sprawl development actually weighed more than their fellow citizens. "We found that U.S. adults living in sprawling counties weigh more, and are more likely to be obese and are more likely to suffer from high blood pressure than are their counterparts in compact counties," the university reported. More than 200,000 people living in 448 counties were studied as part of the research. The average adult living in the most sprawling county was found to weigh 6 pounds more than an adult the same age living in the most compact county. "It may be as a result of the lower level of physical activity they get as part of their daily lives," the researchers concluded, "driving to work, driving to school, driving to lunch, basically driving everywhere."

To combat over-consumption, the Superstore Diet is gaining

151

popularity across America. Calculate roughly how much you spent at superstores this past month, and make the commitment to cut your intake by 25% this month, and 25% each month following until you have weaned yourself gradually from Wal-Mart. Exercise daily your right to shop at stores that do not waste land, locate on the edge of town, and cause severe economic dislocation. Friends don't let friends shop at Wal-Mart.

Working Assets, the socially-responsible long-distance phone carrier, urged its subscribers to send the following Christmas message to Wal-Mart's CEO in 2003:

Dear H. Lee Scott, Jr.,

This holiday season, I pledge not to shop at Wal-Mart, and to ask my friends and families not to buy me gifts from Wal-Mart until the chain:

- pays its one million workers a living wage.
- provides affordable health insurance to its employees
- stops discriminating against women
- stops attacking employees who want to be represented by a union.
- ceases forcing unpaid overtime on its employees
- stops pressuring suppliers to lower their labor costs

The United Church of Christ also urged parishioners to stay out of Wal-Mart. The church singled out Wal-Mart's:

- poor record on discrimination based on gender, race, ethnicity and disability;
- forcing workers to labor "off the clock" without pay;
- staunchly anti-union policies;
- poverty level wages and benefits;
- reliance on sweatshop labor in Third World countries.

The church called upon local congregations everywhere to ask Wal-Mart "to act as a responsible global citizen:"

Wal-Mart could have tremendous positive influence on people in towns and cities all across the U.S. and around the world through the company's interactions with its employees, customers, and supplier firms. But we know that Wal-Mart's record on a range of issues is of extreme concern to many. During this holiday season, we urge you to reflect on Wal-Mart's current practices and policies, and to change those that are unjust and inconsistent with the principles of corporate social responsibility.

More and more people are discovering the darker side of Wal-Mart. In a listener response survey released by *Motley Fool Radio* in March 2002, people were asked, "Has Wal-Mart been good for America?" 38% of the callers said "Yes," 34% said "No," and 29% said it was "tough to say." More than 6 out of 10 listeners had concerns about Wal-Mart's contribution to American life.

We have been colonized by an alien nation of Wal-Martians — but we will eventually take it back. I have taken my cue for personal responsibility from the wife of a Wal-Mart manager, who wrote to me, "If a community doesn't want a store, all they have to do is not shop there!" By using your Right <u>Not</u> to Shop at Wal-Mart, you can help bring down the largest threat to competition and the free market today.

The big box companies themselves like to point out that the battle for customers "will be won in the aisles." David Glass, the former Wal-Mart CEO, has said, "At the end of the day, the only vote that really matters is the consumers'."

If we find ourselves in the aisles of these stores, then we are losing the battle. People ask me, "What is the most powerful single thing I can do as an individual to stop superstores?"

I tell them: "Stay out of the aisles."

The last word here is Sam Walton's: "The customers can fire everybody in our Company. And they can do it by simply spending their money somewhere else."

Also available from **Raphel Marketing**:

*Slam-Dunking Wal-Mart!* by Al Norman
The author gives you instructions on how you can preserve
the qualities of your home town against the arrival of the
megastores.
*(Now in its second major printing)*
Paperback $19.95

*Selling Rules!* by Murray Raphel
Murray summarizes a lifetime of selling success with 52 selling
rules, one for each week of the year. Paperback $14.95

*Crowning the Customer* by Feargal Quinn
More than 60,000 copies have been sold to businesses
all around the world. You'll see how to have customers
"boomerang" and come back again.
Paperback $14.95

*Customer Specific Marketing* by Brian Woolf
Brian shows how "loyalty marketing" can increase business and
reduce marketing expenses.
Hard-bound $29.95

Contact Raphel Marketing:
www.raphel.com
Toll free: 877-386-5925
Fax: 609-347-2455
Mail:    Raphel Marketing
         118 S. Newton Ave.
         Atlantic City, NJ 08401